What people are saying about Sean Feucht...

"In 2020 when the pandemic and riots broke out, I was looking to the spiritual leaders of the Church for insight on what to do and how to respond. Frankly, it was like crickets. No one was saying anything; it's like every church leader was afraid to open his mouth.

"Then I caught wind of Sean Feucht. Here was someone who was actually doing something! I immediately joined him at as many of the worship gatherings as possible, knowing that worship was so key!

"After showing up to several of the gatherings, I got so inspired by what was happening that I decided not to wait for the next Let Us Worship event but decided to rally my friends and family and start worshiping wherever we could. We started in homes and garages and backyards, then started going to the beaches of California. We have been experiencing revival.

"Now I've been to twenty cities across the state, bringing worship and evangelism, and every time, God shows up. There have been dozens of salvations, and baptisms in the ocean. We have seen many delivered of demonic oppression and healed of trauma and physical injury.

"I'm grateful for Sean...and the Let Us Worship Movement. It definitely activated something in me to be bold and to not cower to fear and manipulation, but to take back this land for the Kingdom."

—Joel

"I saw a livestream of you in Portland a year or so ago. It changed my life. I found a church to start going to, I attended your revival in Nashville, and I've followed your live events ever since. I now write the study guide for our little church, and I also publish my writing of faith online. I just wanted to say thank you for getting me out of my shell and into worship with others. Thank you!"

—Jamey

"I joined Sean and thousands of other believers in Washington, D.C., in October 2020 at the National Mall. I booked a last-minute flight, just by myself, and worshipped for three days. It was raining all day; the skies were gloomy and very cold. I was out of my element (I'm from SoCal), however, I have never felt so commissioned to be there at one place with so many other believers.

"I was not attending a church at that time and had not been to church in five years, but after watching what Let Us Worship was doing online, I felt a calling to join fellow worshippers at the U.S. Capitol! I came back with a fire and a confirmation for revival in the cities across America.

"I am convinced we are on the verge of the greatest awakening and know that I was created for a purpose at this moment in time for a reason. I am now leading worship at a church in Valencia, California, where Sean held his Azusa Street 2021 New Year's event!! God is good!"

—Sam

"My family and I came to your worship gathering in Portland, Oregon. It was amazing! We were way up in the front, and two of our three kids were baptized. (The other one had already been baptized.)

"When I saw you up in front...with your kids and your wife, I realized that you put everything on the line to follow God....

"It really hit me when you mentioned that before this year you didn't have the same concern for our nation that you do now. I am very hopeful that many other people like you, especially people in pastoral leadership, will wake up and see what God wants them to do. You mentioned—and you are so right—that people in the Body of Christ have to realize that God is in everything—politics, etc.—and not separate.

"I have been praying for our nation for about eight years with a group of women, and I feel that your story and your leadership are definitely an answer to our prayers."

—Laurie

"I went to the Let Us Worship in Lubbock, Texas, and you guys prayed for women who were trying to have babies. I was one of the ones who raised my hand. My husband and I have been trying for about eight months and I found out a couple days ago that I am pregnant!" 😀🙌

—Camie

"I was at a Let Us Worship last night. I surrendered everything to Jesus. I was set free of a porn addiction and a lifelong struggle with same-sex attraction. As I was being prayed for, I was baptized in the Holy Spirit and prayed in tongues!! Thanks, man, for listening to God!"

—Melissa

"I took my teenagers to Kansas City with a friend and her kids to see Sean live. It was better than I could have imagined. The Holy Spirit was so heavy upon us, you could feel it. I am so, so thankful for Sean, his staff, and the volunteers, and all they are doing in the name of the Lord.

"We pray for Sean and this movement to continue and never end until Jesus comes! Sean brings so much hope everywhere he goes. It is so encouraging to see how the Lord is using him.

"I wish there were more Sean Feuchts rising up for the Lord. Praying there will be.... Thank you for all you are doing!"

—Trisha

"I am a sixty-six-year-old grandma who was saved in the '70s and loved the worship then and coffee house gatherings; the love of Jesus was everywhere. Your zeal and passion have reignited that for me and countless others. We only needed a leader to bring that simmering passion to the surface again.

"Thank you from deep in my soul. Your music keeps me worshipping in my living room with your rallies up here in northern Wisconsin."

—Karen

"I'm sure you get hundreds of messages and have met thousands of people over the past few years. I don't know if you remember this young man. I brought him to your Let Us Worship event in NYC on July 3.

"That night Jesus showed up in such a real and tangible way for Jonathan... his life has been transformed! Since then, Jonathan has renounced his ties to the LBGTQ community, has given his life to Christ, and led his entire family to Christ. And last night he was baptized!

"So was his big brother, AJ. A few months ago, his parents were also baptized in the ocean.

"Jonathan and his family are chasing after God! Jonathan's mother told me all the wonderful things God is doing. God has restored their family and her marriage, and there is now peace, love, and joy in their home."

—Sally

"My husband got SAVED last weekend at the Little Rock event! He has transformed into a new man right before my eyes. It's insane!! God is so good! ♥ Thankful we serve a God who still saves and answers prayers! The harvest is here!!!" 🔥

—Britney

"I accepted Jesus as my Savior, got baptized, got delivered from alcoholism, and broke the generational curse in the heart of New Orleans, one of the most popular drinking cities in the country. I went to New Orleans an alcoholic and came home a former alcoholic."

—Sarah

"I attended your recent meeting in Knoxville, Tennessee, along with my niece, her husband, and their seven foster kids. All seven kids responded to the altar call and five were water baptized. The next day was Easter, and they received Bibles as their gifts.

"Today is Sunday, April 25, 2021, and these kids are picking up the Bible every day and reading it. It is amazing to watch the handiwork of God in this short time. Thank you for hearing clearly and obeying quickly the leading of Holy Spirit to come to East Tennessee, and holy boldness to proclaim the Gospel message!"

—Carla

"The craziest thing just happened! I was watching Sean Feucht on TV and some of the people in the house sat beside me to watch it, too. In the meantime, I saw that they weren't understanding everything since it is in English, so I started translating the livestream just as I do in the crusades. And by the end of it, seven people were converted to Jesus in the house!!!"

—Vicente

"Your three days in Mobile completely changed my family. There really are no words. I have been in the hardest season of my life but finally have true peace. The story would take too long to explain but seeing my former addict son praying with raised hands and seeing his heart change the last few months has been amazing. Your event only deepened our faith and determination to stay in God's will. PLEASE DO NOT STOP WHAT YOU ARE DOING! Our church group of fifteen to twenty who went all three nights will never be the same."

—Erin

"We were at the event tonight and my niece decided to quit cutting! 😭😭😭 Thank you!!!! " 😭🤍🤍🤍

—Martha

"My friend was healed of throat constriction and tightness in his stomach at worship Sunday night in Fort Worth! He has been in pain for a year and a half, and when prayed for, got instantly healed!"

—Connor

"When the call was made for healing in the joints [in Knoxville, Tennessee], I was healed! I had an ACL surgery seventeen years ago and it has been painful to even squat (when I walk sometimes you can hear clicking or popping in my knee). Yesterday, in faith I squatted and there was zero pain, zero sounds of popping or clicking!!!!"

—Elisa

BOLD

BOLD

Moving
Forward in Faith,
Not Fear

SEAN FEUCHT

SALEM
BOOKS

an imprint of Regnery Publishing
Washington, D.C.

Unless otherwise indicated, scripture quotations are taken from the *Holy Bible, New International Version®*, NIV®. Copyright ©1973, 1978, 1984, 2011 by Biblica, Inc.™ Used by permission of Zondervan. All rights reserved worldwide. www.zondervan.com. The "NIV" and "New International Version" are trademarks registered in the United States Patent and Trademark Office by Biblica, Inc.™

Scripture quotations marked ESV are taken from *The Holy Bible, English Standard Version*, copyright © 2001 by Crossway Bibles, a division of Good News Publishers. Used by permission. All rights reserved.

Scripture quotations marked KJV are taken from the *King James Version* of the Bible.

Scripture quotations marked MSG are from *The Message* by Eugene H. Peterson, copyright © 1993, 1994, 1995, 1996, 2000, 2001, 2002. Used by permission of NavPress Publishing Group. All rights reserved.

Scripture quotations marked NASB are taken from the (NASB®) *New American Standard Bible®*, Copyright © 1960, 1971, 1977, 1995, 2020 by The Lockman Foundation. Used by permission. All rights reserved. www.lockman.org.

Manuscript prepared by Rick Killian, Killian Creative, Boulder, Colorado. www.killiancreative.com.

Salem Books™ is a trademark of Salem Communications Holding Corporation. Regnery® and its colophon is a registered trademark of Salem Communications Holding Corporation.

Cataloging-in-Publication data on file with the Library of Congress

ISBN: 978-1-68451-367-3
eISBN: 978-1-68451-368-0

Library of Congress Control Number: 2022937272

Published in the United States by
Salem Books
An Imprint of Regnery Publishing
A Division of Salem Media Group
Washington, D.C.
www.SalemBooks.com

Manufactured in the United States of America

10 9 8 7 6 5 4 3 2 1

Books are available in quantity for promotional or premium use. For information on discounts and terms, please visit our website: www.SalemBooks.com.

The light shines in the darkness,
and the darkness has not overcome it.

—John 1:5

Courage is not simply one of the virtues but
the form of every virtue at the testing point, which means
at the point of highest reality.

—C. S. Lewis

CONTENTS

INTRODUCTION

*There are things for which an uncompromising stand
is worthwhile.*

—Dietrich Bonhoeffer

The only way truth can be silenced is when no one is bold enough to speak it.

We're told today that we live in a post-Christian, and even a post-truth, society. There are no absolutes. What science can't confirm as real doesn't exist—and even what science seems sure about can be called into question. Ancient wisdom is long past its expiration date. Faith—and truth—are really up to the individual. And "the God, the universe, or whatever you want to call it" is a legitimate way to begin a "spiritual, but not religious" conversation.

And people call *me* crazy.

Don't get me wrong. There are a lot of good things about what is happening in our current generation. It's great to see the hunger for authenticity and meaningful connection, the movement away from consumerism and materialism, the embracing of the diversity with which God created us, a heart for the oppressed and forgotten, the rejection of hypocrisy and corruption, and the desire to help others and close the gap between the haves and have nots. I believe, at their core, these have been seeded throughout the great political experiment that is the United States. This began with one of our founding documents, the Declaration of Independence, which stated in 1776 that "all men are created equal and endowed by their Creator with certain unalienable rights." I believe our success as a nation—and as an example to the value of democracy around the world—depends on us living these values in revolutionary new ways.

Yet somehow, these values have become a battle cry not for reconciliation, justice, and unity, but for people to be canceled, for violent protests that turn into riots destroying property and creating mayhem, for lawlessness and anarchy in the face of civil authority, and for silencing the voices of anyone who disagrees. Dissent seems to be at an all-time high in America today, and there is a tremendous fight raging to control the narrative about what is happening, regardless of actual facts. Each side blames the other for it, and the divisiveness is tangible. Throw in a pandemic, further racial tensions, a scold war on social media that is out of control, and mainstream media outlets that profit more from stirring up conflict than from bringing peace, and you have a recipe for utter chaos.

Unless, of course, more of us are willing to stand up in boldness and voice a different narrative—one that heals instead of injures, reconciles instead of divides, forgives instead of cancels, delivers instead of enslaves, and saves instead of condemns.

And the only message I know that will do that is the Gospel of Jesus Christ.

In a time when people are trying to shout each other down, I think it's time we flipped the script and started shouting up.

But that takes a quality that is hard to come by in an age that is demanding conformity to a certain set of selfish, manipulative, polarizing values. It's tough when governments are mandating seclusion and trying to silence the Church. It's tough when you're threatened and thrown into self-doubt, uncertainty, and fear.

The only answer is to return all the more strongly to what we are certain of. It demands a return to the truth. It demands a fresh embracing of values we know will last, like faith, hope, and love.

It demands, in essence, the willingness to be *bold*.

Over the last two years, without leaving the United States, my family and I have faced the greatest opposition we have ever experienced, and that is saying something for a missionary who has taken the Gospel to places where it is completely illegal to preach it, like Afghanistan, Saudi Arabia, the frontline of the war with ISIS, and North Korea. Never have I been called out the way I have been in this time, accused of so many different things, or lost so many friends.

At the same time, never have I seen revival like what we have experienced, the power of the Gospel to save in a time of need, or seen lives changed, darkness vanquished, or fears dethroned. The last two years have been a testament to the power of the simple Gospel and what can happen if God's people will simply gather, lift up the name of the Lord, and pray, regardless of the forces standing against them.

In the last two years, the journey of Let Us Worship has created a moment to allow the Church to step into this kind of boldness and be a bright light in a very dark time. We have already seen so much of God's goodness and faithfulness, and we feel like we're only getting started. This book is about that journey and the things we have learned so far along the way. I share it as a shout-out to God and what He can do if we would simply be the people He's called us to be.

It's time to be confident in our assured salvation. It's time for us to be confident in our growing relationships and love for Jesus. It's time to find a new boldness in our faith, our prayers, our worship, our missions, our leadership, our love, our justice, our obedience, our gratitude, our identity, our witness, our unity, our legacy, and our hope.

We are the generation put on the earth for such a time as this. Despite how crazy things in our culture, society, and the world may seem, we were fashioned for this moment. Each of us has a part to play. My prayer and desire are that the following pages will help encourage and strengthen you in your part of being *bold*.

Sean Feucht
February 1, 2022

ONE

BOLD FAITH

Faithless is he that says farewell
when the road darkens.

—J. R. R. Tolkien, *The Fellowship of the Ring*

I t was Super Tuesday, March 3, 2020, when my bid for California's District 3 congressional seat ended with an abruptness that left me reeling and questioning myself for weeks. I had done everything my advisors said I was supposed to do. I raised the money. I burned the candle at both ends. I traveled across America and California raising support. I spent endless hours studying the issues so I could speak intelligently about them, and I took all the media interviews I could get.

In the process, I met some incredible people and received some amazing encouragement. I was sure I could make it through the primaries and on to the general election. That would further embolden me to make my case for change before the November elections. I mean, since I look nothing like a politician, I looked the part for "change," you know? As a thirty-something, long-haired alternative to the status quo, I was sure to get the millennial vote. As a worship leader, I was sure to get the church vote. And in a district that was largely rural except for Sacramento, as a Republican, I felt I represented fresh hope.

How could I not at least finish in the top two in the primaries?

But I was completely wrong.

Instead, I lost to the other Republican in the race by half—and received less than a quarter of the votes of the front-running, incumbent Democrat.

I was both dumbfounded and heartbroken. What I had been relentlessly pursuing with all of my time and focus for six months was suddenly just *over*.

What had I been thinking?

As I drove four hours back home from our campaign office in Fairfield with my family to our home in Redding that brisk March night, no one said a word. My wife, Kate, and I were both silent. Over the years, we had talked through some of the most difficult topics a couple could face, from infertility to the risks of taking our family on missions trips to some of the most dangerous places in the world—but on that drive home, neither of us could give voice to the chaos of emotions and thoughts inside of us.

Below the surface, I was seething with rage, anguish, and pain. I was angry at what I had put my family through. Kate had taken the brunt of it with me—personal attacks, character slurs, long-time friends thinking I had lost my mind who suddenly refused to return our calls. I had traveled relentlessly and missed so many of my kids' activities—and *for what?*

I was angry at myself, and I was angry at God.

In my heart, I cried out, *What are You doing? My life is completely blown up! I let everyone who supported me down. Who's ever going to trust me enough to give and join our ministry again?*

I'm normally a very positive, hopeful person. I'm as driven as they come. Typically, I'm like, "I'll take this mountain today, and on to the next tomorrow." But the morning after I lost that election, I could not get out of bed. I could not face reality. I had failed, and that was all on me. I was so devastated, I honestly did not believe I would ever even lead worship again.

I have a friend who works with hedge funds in New York, and since I have a business degree, I started thinking about giving him a call. Maybe he had a place for me. I was ready to pull us up and start all over again on the other side of the country.

Had I missed God in running for office? Or worse, did God set me up for this? Was He trying to teach me some obscure, painful lesson? Or had I just made a mistake?

I couldn't even pick up the phone for the next three days.

But I didn't have time to wallow.

Within days of Super Tuesday, the first case of COVID-19 in the district where I had run was discovered. In fact, it wasn't far from the Solano County Courthouse in Fairfield, California, where I had originally signed the papers to declare my candidacy.

A couple mornings later, I remember lying in bed, looking at my phone, reading yet another headline about the virus. I turned to Kate and said, "I think this is going to change our lives forever."

She looked at me. "What are you talking about?"

"This virus," I said. "There's something about it. It's going to change things."

As I said that, my thoughts went back to the last sermon I'd given in 2019. It was during a prayer gathering in a church on Wall Street in New York City, the day before New Year's Eve. My family and our global Burn 24-7 worship community were ending our annual fast and had gathered together to see what God would impress upon us for 2020.

I was overwhelmed in the midst of my election run, and I'm sure I was preoccupied with that, but the verse that came to me was Revelation 1:17:

> When I saw him, I fell at his feet as though dead. Then he placed his right hand on me and said: "Do not be afraid. I am the First and the Last."

Not having anything else, I ended up preaching on that verse. I think it resonated with me because I'd been facing a lot of fears in the midst of the congressional race. The Apostle John saw a vision of Jesus, and then he fell at His feet as though dead.

Jesus's response? The first words out of His mouth were, *"Do not be afraid. I am the First and the Last."*

As I lay there in bed, I asked Kate if she remembered me preaching that. She did. I told her, "I don't know what's going to happen in 2020, but I feel like this is a verse that we're going to need."

I thought about it some more, trying to remember what I had said that New Year's Eve night three months prior. John hadn't even cracked into the meat of the apocalyptic, end-of-the-world Book of Revelation yet. He hadn't seen the horses' bridles bathed in blood yet. He had yet to see any of the seals broken open or curses poured out. All he'd seen was Jesus, and he was already overwhelmed. John already couldn't deal with it; he was literally floored.

And Jesus said to him, *"Don't be afraid. I am the First and the Last."* In other words, "Don't worry, it all begins and ends with Me. I am the author of the whole story. Nothing will happen that I haven't written."

In my New York City sermon, I remember saying that it didn't matter what we faced in 2020. Whatever came, we needed to resist fear. That was the main point of what I preached.

Then, because I had run for office and made friends on the inside of government—state legislators and other officials—I started getting texts from them saying we should go to the store immediately to stock up on essentials (like flour, rice, and toilet paper) because California Governor Gavin Newsom was going to shut everything down the next day. We were facing the first twenty-one-day attempt of the COVID-19 pandemic to keep people at home and "slow the spread."

I'm sure you remember what happened next as well as I do. People started going nuts. There was a run on toilet paper and dry goods. Whole shelves in the supermarkets were cleared of canned goods, baking supplies and other staples, and things stayed that way for weeks.

Fear was gripping everyone. It was itself a pandemic.

Then, just like my friends had said, everything was shut down. On March 19, Newsom issued a mandatory statewide shelter-in-place order.

It didn't seem like a big deal at the time, other than we were suddenly isolated and it didn't leave me any room to work out my pain from losing the election with my local church and friends. Kate and I were alone for that, but really, we were fine and, like everyone else, we wanted to do everything we could to slow the spread of the virus and get things back to the way they had been.

But at the same time, it was crazy—remember? We watched videos about how to properly sanitize our groceries after bringing them home. Kate made me take my shoes off before entering the house because people were saying you might track COVID into your home. Churches had to pivot quickly to begin holding services online. It all just seemed like the right thing to do for everyone's safety.

Then it went on...and on. I had twenty international trips planned with our ministry, and they all got canceled. Kate looked at me and said, "Maybe this is a God thing. Maybe He's giving us a sabbatical. We need the rest."

I agreed. "Yeah, maybe we just need to heal and rest and seek God for the next season. Let's just tread water for a little bit, you know, to give us time to see which direction to go from here."

So we did—to a point.

That was when the discrepancies started to get to me. Places of worship were deemed "non-essential" and were mandated to stay closed while casinos, strip clubs, and marijuana dispensaries remained open. This felt like hypocrisy at best and a blatant attack against the Church at worst. Not only that, but by July, with no end to the mandated closings in sight, a couple of churches sued the state of California for violating their First Amendment rights to gather and practice their faith.

Having run for political office, I got to peek behind the veil of politics there. I was able to see how staying in power often means using that power to silence opposition in hidden ways. The public faces and the private actions of many I met, even those who were supposed to be on my side, were very different. If there was a loophole to be used to gain an edge, most of them exploited it. Politicians worked the system to their advantage and manipulated opponents and the rules to get what they wanted. Though I also met some really great, honest leaders, corner-cutting and "twisting the rules to take advantage of opportunities" was common practice on both sides of the aisle.

Then in late May, America exploded over the tragic death of George Floyd while in police custody on May 25, 2020. Perhaps because so many of us were sheltering at home and paying far more attention to news cycles than ever before, people reacted to this injustice more profoundly than any story involving police violence since April 1992, when riots broke out in L.A. after white police officers accused of beating Rodney King, a black man, were acquitted.

This time, however, the reactions were not localized. More than two thousand cities and towns in more than sixty nations joined in the protests. Violence, arson, vandalism, and looting in more than thirty states and Washington, D.C. between May 26 and June 8 caused approximately $2 billion in damages—the highest recorded damage from civil disorder in U.S. history, far surpassing the previous record set during the 1992 Los Angeles riots.[1] By November, more than fourteen thousand people had been arrested and twenty-five had lost their lives. The downtown areas of Portland, Oregon, and Seattle, Washington were engulfed in constant protests, as were other cities across the nation.

Left-wing groups organized under the flag of Antifa-staged protests that were at times peaceful but too often not. "Woke" society and Black Lives Matter (BLM) flooded social media with their condemnatory statements against law enforcement and organized marches across the country. While state and local governments were asking folks to "shelter at home," protest groups were taking to the streets, shouting at the top of their lungs, and cities were required to protect their constitutional rights to do so. Police watched from the sidelines as protestors screamed "defund the police." In early June, the Capitol Hill Autonomous Zone (CHAZ) was created around Seattle's Cal Anderson Park, encompassing about six blocks of the neighborhood, and was declared a "police-free" zone. Seattle police actually abandoned their East Precinct, which was within the area behind barriers—a move that was followed by mayhem.

Seeing this on the news every evening, it started to bug me even more that churches were being threatened with fines and their members imprisoned should they gather, but these protestors were left to run wild with little condemnation from local officials. Not only that, but people gathered by the hundreds in big box stores, while churches remained closed. Bars, marijuana dispensaries, and strip clubs were deemed "essential businesses" and allowed to remain open as well.

Was there something behind this strong stance against churches? Was this a desire for those who didn't agree with the opinions of Christians to essentially silence them using COVID-19 as an excuse? Yes, definitely—public safety was a concern and restrictions made sense to a certain extent, but why weren't they being applied evenly? Why were people allowed to gather for ungodly things, but the godly couldn't be together to worship and pray to God?

I wasn't looking for a fight. I'd already stepped into the ring and taken my licks. I wasn't anxious to do it again—not any time soon, anyway. But as I saw these things happening, they started getting under my skin.

Then we started to hear about the rising rates of depression, anxiety, and suicide among the isolated. I started to see this as a season when the churches were needed more than ever—but now they were closed. How were online churches going to help these people? Were the lost going to somehow be reached through an email campaign? That didn't make any sense.

Frankly, it really rubbed me the wrong way, but what could I do about it? I would go back and forth over it in my mind, thinking, *I just need to live with it until this all blows over.*

Then, in early July, the state of California announced:

> Places of worship must...discontinue indoor singing and chanting activities and limit indoor attendance to 25 percent of building capacity or a maximum of 100 attendees, whichever is lower.[2]

In other words, church members couldn't gather by the dozens to worship God with their voices, while protestors had protected rights to march in thousands, take over areas of cities, and shout profanities and anti-government and anti-law enforcement slogans at the top of their lungs. Christians were being told they couldn't practice one of the essential activities of their faith—singing praise and worship to God together as a body.

That was the last straw for me. I could not sit back and just watch this happen.

Shaken to Our Core

When the global pandemic hit in 2020, it shook every nation of the world to its core. Trial, tragedy, and trauma have a way of exposing who we truly are as people and what we really believe in.

As our world went insane around us—clearing store shelves as if we were in the first stages of the zombie apocalypse, voicing our disdain for people wearing (or not wearing) masks, constantly checking our phones for updates on the latest variant, and the like—we were given a choice. Would we acquiesce to the heightened levels of fear, anxiety, desperation, and drama in the world around us? Or would we shout all the louder that our God is real, Jesus is Lord, and everything begins and ends with Him?

Don't misunderstand me. Some have accused me of being a pandemic denier, but that's not true. My sisters and my family are in the medical field, and I've lost people close to me to COVID-19. I know it's real. I've seen what it can do. I've experienced the ripples of the devastation and grief it has produced. My mindset, as it developed through March into July of that year, shifted in a significant way. While fully realizing the seriousness of COVID-19 and seeing loved ones and friends die from it, a parallel realization dawned on me: Fear was gripping everyone, including Christians, and the confusion that fear brought was causing division and chaos inside the church.

So for me, the battle to defeat COVID-19 was being waged on several fronts:

1. A climate of fear that descended on everyone, including the Church
2. The very real health threat it posed to millions
3. The widely differing ways state and local governments reacted to the pandemic
4. The fact that churches seemed to be singled out unfairly for the reasons I outlined above (e.g., strip clubs and dispensaries were open, but churches were not)

But here is where I eventually landed: If God is who we say He is—who we so confidently sang in church that He is before the world got turned upside down—how should the Body of Christ be reacting to all of this? Had God suddenly changed, or was it us? While we didn't have much control over which mandates and rules our governing leaders imposed on us, *what could we control* as the Body of Christ, and how should we respond?

Before the pandemic, did we simply base our lives more on the conveniences and cultural currents of living in one of the most developed nations in the world? Did our positive platitudes and confessions of faith come too easily? Or were they so shallow that when the winds of the pandemic began to rage, our faith was picked up along with the house built on sand and blown into the sea?

Again, it's not that the fear we've faced in these times hasn't been real. We have been shaken. Every stable element of our previous lives has been disrupted and laid bare. We have been isolated, given too much time to think in many cases, and need to sincerely process the worry and fear we've been experiencing.

So again, what God has impressed on me is this question: When it comes right down to it, how should people of *bold faith* react?

Bold faith is not a fluffy Christian catchphrase. Hebrews 11:1 (KJV) calls it "the *substance* of things hoped for, the evidence of things not seen." Faith carries weight. It is definable and attainable. It is the inner grit and resolve that makes you refuse to let go of what you truly believe in. It is a solid foundation you can build a life upon.

Every one of us has taken a journey of self-discovery in the last season and discovered the *substance* of who we are. As the storms of the pandemic came—and have kept coming and coming—we were left to grapple with whether our foundations were being built on the sand or on the rock. If we've been found wanting, we have the choice to either give it up or double down.

Every nation around the world has been deeply affected by this virus, but what we've faced in the U.S. is very different than the challenges in other parts of the world. In the early months of the pandemic, I remember receiving frantic phone calls and WhatsApp messages from the leaders of the Light A Candle project—a missions organization I founded that includes an expansive child sponsorship program in India.

"We cannot get food to the children. They are going hungry and face certain death unless God intervenes! Pray for us! Remember your family in the most remote parts of India."

These were messages from the pastors and leaders of the more than 970 children we helped rescue from the worst imaginable circumstances over the past few years: temple prostitution, child labor camps, and poverty on levels we cannot even fathom in the

West. But God opened the door for us to help them, and they were now in homes, orphanages, and safe houses where they were being fed, educated, and loved by true heroes of the faith—unknown on Earth, but famous in Heaven.

The lockdowns across India were severe, and the government flexed all its muscle to quell anyone who dared to defy curfew orders. The repercussions for breaking the rules were so brutal that even being seen on the streets walking, biking, or riding motorbikes could get you beaten severely by the police. Government officials disrupted all our people's usual routes, travel, and strategy for getting food, clothes, and supplies to our sponsored children.

And as a result, they were going hungry. Supply chain problems were keeping regular shipments from them. I remember several urgent phone calls with our team eleven time zones away discussing these matters. As we formulated strategies and assessed the risks of breaking the law in order to keep our children alive, one of the pastors said something that will forever stick with me. Hearing his desperation over the phone changed my life.

"Pastor Sean, they keep telling us there is no way to get the food to our kids and that we must let them starve," he said. "But we are a people of faith. We are bold people, and we will not stop! We will never stop!"

And stop they never did. Through many lessons of trial and error, our leaders found the exact times when the least police would be out on certain street corners. They dressed in all black and drove motorbikes strapped with food and supplies hundreds of miles through the night to village after village, week after week, until every child's need was met.

If that's not doubling down on your faith in God, I don't know what is. The substance of their faith was on display as they saved countless lives through their selfless actions.

The call to bold faith is more than a concept, an idea, or an aphorism. It has to be lived out to be real. Many who have gone before us embraced this high calling of living by bold faith to their dying days.

I've witnessed this reality not just from biblical heroes and friends overseas, but also firsthand with my father. After receiving the unexpected and horrifying news in early 2010 that a Stage 4 glioblastoma tumor was growing rapidly on the left side of his brain, my dad stepped into a measure of faith that I had never seen in him before. I know now that it must have always been there, but it was this trial and the uncertainty that unearthed the gritty fight beneath his perpetually calm and composed demeanor.

Being a doctor himself for more than thirty years, he understood the diagnosis and the gravity of the situation more than any of us. Yet while facing all of that, he somehow remained undeterred in his belief that God had the power to heal, save, and deliver him from it.

He told me several times that even if he was not healed, he would never allow the diagnosis of cancer to steal the foundation of his faith. He faced every doctor appointment, every grim statistic, and every chemotherapy treatment with a resolve that God's power could overcome any and every obstacle that stood in his way.

This was the substance that produced a boldness I will never forget. I remember sitting next to him as he breathed deeply in his weakened state after the intense cancer treatments, and we worshipped as I lightly strummed my guitar in his living room. Tears streamed down my face as I watched my father raise his hands to Heaven and give God glory while his body was suffering in cancer's violent clutches. He seemed unfazed while carrying a quiet confidence and a sincere devotion to the Lord.

This was my most significant up-close-and-personal encounter with bold faith. Something was imparted to me in these lonely, beautiful, and sobering nights together with my dad. Heaven kissed Earth and I could almost feel the angels' bewilderment as they witnessed his persistence and affectionate desire to surrender his entire life, will, and emotions to Jesus.

We are not called to live in fear; we are called to live by faith. We are called to love the world around us like Jesus did. 1 John 4:18 tells us that "perfect love drives out fear, because fear has to do with punishment. The one who fears is not made perfect in love."

Just as courage is not the absence of fear, but acting boldly in the face of it, so faith does not deny circumstances, but overcomes them through wisdom, perseverance, and confidence that our God is in charge and His will *will* be done.

After losing my race for Congress, I thought it was time to sit on the sideline for a bit and heal—but I came to see that wasn't God's plan. The mission that had encouraged me to run for Congress hadn't changed: America still needs voices of faith to stand up for what is right. Yes, the risks of the virus and ungodly opposition are real, but faith is our calling, our inheritance, and our destiny as people of God. We cannot stop proclaiming the

Gospel and God's desire to transform our lives for the better. More than any authority on the earth, Jesus deserves our honor and praise. He's calling for us to do these things in bold faith. This is our invitation.

How are we going to answer that call?

TWO

BOLD PRAYERS

You do not have because you do not ask God.

—James 4:2

Many—inside the church and out—have thought I was crazy for how I reacted to Gavin Newsom's edict that there should be no singing in church, but you've got to understand where I was coming from.

First of all, I am a worship leader who has been called to take the Gospel into some of the most dangerous places on Earth. If you've read my book *Brazen*, you know that as a teenager returning from my first mission trip, I listed the five most dangerous places in the world on sticky notes and then started praying that God would open doors to each one. I've now been to four of them. Plus, I've taken my family—Kate and our four kids, Keturah, Malachi, Ezra, and Zion—into places like Indonesia during a period of serious unrest, and twice into wartime Iraq. I've been taken to the front lines by the Kurdish Peshmerga and seen ISIS flags flying over their camps with my own eyes. I've had AK-47s held to my head by thieves in Uganda and nearly died at least two other times on outreaches.

I don't say this to impress you. I share it because almost all the activity we do in missions overseas defies the governments there and is often dangerous for numerous reasons. With my teams, God has opened the door for me to take the light of His Word into some of the darkest places on Earth—and we went to those places specifically *because* of that darkness. People support our outreaches to go to these places and are encouraged when we come back and tell them what God does there. He has shown up every time.

So when we break the law overseas because foreign governments condemn Christian worship and evangelization, what are we to do when the laws of our own nation forbid the same practices? I mean, thousands of people were crammed inside every big box store across California, yet churches "singing" together once a week was the greatest "superspreader" threat? It was ludicrous. It felt like a total power play to me.

Then, as tighter and tighter restrictions closed in around us in California, I started getting texts from connections I had made in those dangerous places overseas asking me things like, "What's going on with your government? I thought you had religious freedom, and they're saying that you can't gather, you can't preach without a mask, and now that you can't sing? *What are you going to do, brother?*"

I've got to tell you, there was no way I could do nothing.

The day Gavin Newsom issued the mandate forbidding singing was Wednesday, July 3, 2020. I will never forget that moment! We quickly launched an online Freedom to Worship petition and called it "Let Us Worship." (It gained some momentum online and garnered tens of thousands of signatures in just a few days.) I also felt we needed to do more to put feet to the prayers and proclamations expressed in the petition. It could not just be an email we passed around and signed with our names. We needed to have skin in the game. We needed to take a stand for what we believed and show the world we were not going to let the government remove our God-given right to worship!

So we posted on our website that we would have a spontaneous prayer meeting on the Golden Gate Bridge in the middle of the day on July 9. One of the gates in Jerusalem that leads to the Temple Mount is called the Golden Gate, and it was through this that Jesus entered Jerusalem. The bridge seemed a fitting and symbolic place to gather and invite God into our situation as the "Golden Gate" of the West.

We had no idea if anyone would show up. However, without our even knowing it, God was forming a "Gideon's army" to stand and boldly pray in response to the worship ban. About four hundred people miraculously gathered to join us, parking a mile from the bridge and walking to meet us. About two hundred showed up on the north end and two hundred more on the south. The bridge is a mile and a half long, so once gathered, we began the trek towards the middle at the same time.

As we started on our way, a policeman pulled up on a motor-cycle and asked me what we were doing.

I said, "Hey, we actually came to the bridge today because we want to pray for the city."

He looked at me, and I could see tears starting to well up in his eyes. "Man," he said. "What took you so long?"

It turned out he was one of a handful of officers going back and forth on the bridge on 24/7 suicide patrol. He mentioned that the Golden Gate is the most popular suicide spot in the nation; the police were doing everything they could to save lives, but it wasn't enough.

Immediately he got on his radio, and over a dozen police cars and motorcycles responded to his call. They ended up blocking off a lane of northbound traffic on the bridge to give us more room to worship. All we had was a little battery-powered speaker and a few acoustic guitars, but it was all we needed. People were hungry and ready to worship together.

I was amazed by what was happening. I felt like people in America needed to see something that gave them hope. My assistant, Whitney, was with us, so I asked her if she could do a Facebook live post sharing the raw and gritty moment we were in. In a matter of minutes, it started going viral. Networks started recording our feed and showed it on their newscasts. That footage was eventually seen by over hundreds of thousands. People couldn't believe what we were doing.

The group that gathered was extremely diverse as well. There were black pastors, Asian pastors, and Hispanic pastors. There were immigrants. People from the heart of San Francisco and people from the suburbs around the Bay Area. Some had flags. I handed the mic around as different pastors wanted to pray. It was intense. The Church showed up and we shouted out to Heaven together. We called on God to start a new Jesus People Movement in the same state He had done it in in the late 1960s.

As we started to worship and pray, it was as if we exited the current reality and circumstances that surrounded us and began to speak from a heavenly place. We were declaring, "The Western gate is open in America..."

One of the pastors prayed:

> We pray an open heaven over northern California. We say, "Open the gate so that the King of Glory would come in." Father, we are praying a blessing over this city tonight. We declare it is Your city. We declare You are for this city. You are for the people in this city. And, Lord, tonight, we are declaring, stating, and believing for the greatest outpouring of the Holy Spirit You have ever experienced on this city and on northern California.[1]

We stood on the Golden Gate Bridge and asked for God to meet us in our need and pour out His Spirit again on our land. In many ways, it was as simple as that.

But what it launched was anything but simple.

The Simplicity of Prayer

I find it interesting that the disciples never asked Jesus how to launch a successful ministry or a thriving business. They never asked Jesus how to start and grow a church. We never read of them asking how to raise support or how they could create a brand and market it successfully to build their ministry. They walked, talked, ate, ministered, and lived life for almost three years with Jesus, but they never asked Him such questions. They saw it all. Even though Jesus was likely successful in all those things in some form or another, the disciples never asked Him how to do any of them.

Instead, they asked Him to teach them how to pray.

The disciples witnessed Jesus withdrawing on many occasions to be alone with His Father in prayer. He would spend entire nights on a mountain to escape the crowds, busyness, and distractions of ministry to be alone with His Father to speak with Him. Prayer was His solace, His time of strengthening and recalibration. The disciples knew that the connection and intimacy He had with His Father was the source of Jesus's wisdom, authority, and direction.

His response to their pleas went like this:

> This, then, is how you should pray:
> "Our Father in heaven,
> hallowed be your name,
> your kingdom come,
> your will be done,
> on earth as it is in heaven.
> Give us today our daily bread.
> And forgive us our debts,
> as we also have forgiven our debtors.
> And lead us not into temptation,
> but deliver us from the evil one." (Matthew 6:9–13)

We tend to overcomplicate things that were purposely designed to be simple. Prayer is one of those things. We are told numerous times throughout Scripture that fancy words and verbosity are not what moves the heart of God. It is not a show or performance before others. Prayer is not trying to convince an angry Judge to do something He does not want to do. Instead, prayer is honest conversation with a loving Father who longs to hear from His children and meet their needs in the way that is best for them.

But also notice the priorities in the model prayer Jesus gave His disciples (and subsequently us). First come the words: *"Our Father in heaven."* While we take it somewhat for granted that God is our Father in the Church today, it was a revolutionary concept at the time. One of the bones religious leaders picked with Jesus was His calling God "My Father." (John 5:18 tells us it was one of the reasons the Jewish leaders wanted to kill Him.) The idea of going to God and calling Him "Abba, Father," was nothing short of sacrilegious to them, but it was one of the greatest revelations Jesus came to the earth to give.

For Jesus, prayer began in acknowledging that Father-child relationship—that we don't come to God as strangers or plaintiffs, but as daughters and sons, children of the King, and joint-heirs with Christ. That fact alone is worth a great deal of meditation. No matter how many times you may hear it, it takes a while to get that realization down into your soul.

Second, Jesus instructs us to pray, "Hallowed be your name." Prayer goes from acknowledging relationship into praise. (Which we'll dive into more in the next chapter.)

Third comes the first petition or request. It is, "Your kingdom come, your will be done, on Earth as it is in Heaven." The most important request we have as children of Heaven is asking that in every possible way, this place (the earth) will look like His place (Heaven). The commission from Jesus in teaching us this is that we should pray with confidence that His kingdom would manifest and His will would be done on the earth. What a powerful and stirring thought!

From there, we can present to God our other needs and ask that we be protected from evil.

Yes, prayer requires faith and courage, but it is built on these simple principles. We should never complicate it. It is coming to God and acknowledging simple truths that usher us into His throne room:

1. He is our Father, and we are His beloved children,
2. He is worthy of praise, and
3. Our first and foremost request of Him should always be that His will be done on Earth as it is in Heaven, ushering in His Kingdom.

Jesus continued to build upon this theme with other things He taught about prayer.

Therefore I tell you, whatever you ask for in prayer, believe that you have received it, and it will be yours. (Mark 11:24)

If you believe, you will receive whatever you ask for in prayer. (Matthew 21:22)

And John added in his first epistle:

This is the confidence we have in approaching God: that if we ask anything according to His will, He hears us. And if we know that He hears us—whatever we ask—we know that we have what we asked of Him. (1 John 5:14–15)

Heaven comes into agreement and alignment with us when we pray according to His will—according to His promises. This is how you know that this boldness is not for your own ego or to prove anything to anyone: it is purely to be obedient and receive the pleasure of our Father. It is my lifelong desire that my prayer life would be in such congruence with His heart that I would feel the agreement of Heaven like the disciples did.

None of us is greater than our prayer life—including Jesus. And if Jesus needed a quality prayer life, how much more do we?

Prayer is the place of connection with God. It is the detox to our obsessively busy culture. It is the seat of our realignment with Heaven. It is the source of our spiritual authority and the place of our utmost clarity. History belongs to the intercessors. It has always been that way.

Take, for example, what Israel was facing when Psalm 2 was written. The psalmist laments that the forces of darkness are mounting a full-on assault against the plans and purposes of God, which feels more and more like the day we are now living in.

> Why do the nations conspire
> and the peoples plot in vain?
> The kings of the earth rise up
> and the rulers band together
> against the Lord and against his anointed, saying,

"Let us break their chains
and throw off their shackles." (Psalm 2:1–3)

A great showdown is taking place. The armies of the world have summoned their strength against the Lord and His hosts. And in the midst of this end-of-the-age battle, a clear command is given:

Ask me,
and I will make the nations your inheritance,
the ends of the earth your possession. (Psalm 2:8)

What a bold declaration to be given at such a crucial hour of battle! Not only is there a radical joy and gloating over the enemy's imminent failure, but then there is a challenge to *ask* for the nations when they rise up in opposition!

James echoes this quite simply and elegantly:

You do not have because you do not ask God. When you ask, you do not receive, because you ask with wrong motives, that you may spend what you get on your pleasures. (James 4:2–3)

This is why we should pray according to the things God has already promised us, as much as possible echoing Scripture and its intended purpose. We cannot pray His words and not be heard by Heaven.

So is my word that goes out from my mouth:
It will not return to me empty,
but will accomplish what I desire
and achieve the purpose for which I sent it. (Isaiah 55:11)

When my staff, my family, and I travel to war zones, red light districts, or cities of strife, turmoil, and destruction, we always train the intercessors and worshippers to contend according to Scripture. Isaiah 54 is one of our favorites for this. It speaks of the coming glory and growth God promised Israel and instructs us to sing out and prepare for what the Lord will do, if we would only ask Him. The story of this chapter has been a guidepost for us in seasons and situations when we are facing something contradictory to our prayers. It plainly states not to accept what we see with our eyes, but to turn to God and call on Him for redemption, restoration, and Kingdom advancement. It begins with a song and a shout:

Sing, barren woman,
you who never bore a child;
burst into song, shout for joy,
you who were never in labor;
because more are the children of the desolate woman
than of her who has a husband. (Isaiah 54:1)

In such moments and spaces, we must *sing it* before we *see it*. When we face the reality of our situation, we cannot afford to dumb down our prayers to match "reasonable expectations." Praying from Heaven to Earth—rather than from Earth to Heaven—we can do what Abraham did, calling *"those things which be not as though they were"* (Romans 4:17 KJV).

The passage never gives us permission to complain, whine, or be dismayed when we are facing insurmountable odds. We must sing in the face of the impossible and call God's promises out of the faith realm and into the world we live in.

Not only does this song of the Lord from Isaiah 54 build our faith and turn our eyes from our circumstance to Him, but it opens the door for increase! The very next verses show that our prayers are the catalyst to partner us with the resources and provision of Heaven.

> Enlarge the place of your tent,
> stretch your tent curtains wide,
> do not hold back;
> lengthen your cords,
> strengthen your stakes.
> For you will spread out to the right and to the left;
> your descendants will dispossess nations
> and settle in their desolate cities. (Isaiah 54:2–3)

In the face of barrenness, hardship, and unfulfilled promises, our prayers and proclamations attract breakthrough. When oppositions arise and powers seek to silence us, we must lean all the more into our God and ask for Him to do what only He can do, just like the Church did with the bold prayers in the book of Acts.

A courageously praying church was the primary outflow of the upper-room moment that launched the Church in Acts 1 and 2. The disciples were facing the highest level of threats, violence, and intimidation seen in the New Testament and had many reasons for despair—and yet they did not shy away or give in to fear. Prayer was the source of their strength and the catalyst for their movement.

Only a few chapters later, in Acts 4, we read that Peter and John were arrested as they preached that Jesus was resurrected from the dead. They had become a target a short time earlier for healing a lame beggar in the name of Jesus. They were thrown into jail for the night and brought before the Sanhedrin the next day. When the religious leaders saw their resolve to continue to proclaim the name of Jesus, they threatened them and then released them. The two men returned to the other believers to tell what happened and to lead the Church in prayer for an increase of boldness!

> Now, Lord, consider their threats and enable your servants to speak your word with great boldness. Stretch out your hand to heal and perform signs and wonders through the name of your holy servant Jesus. (Acts 4:29–30)

Can you imagine? After enduring a night in prison and a total dressing down by their culture's prominent leaders, instead of yielding, they prayed for an extra measure of boldness to fill them so they could get in even more trouble!

Such prayers are often the exact opposite of what we pray in Western churches. Self-preservation and safety can often be our biggest prayers and our greatest goals. But the first-century Church prayed almost the exact opposite. They deeply desired a greater brashness to stand against the resistance they faced every day. They knew that without embodying courage, they could not deliver the truth and stand strong in the face of such adversity. They were not trying to escape the circumstances, but were asking for the strength to endure them and continue to increase the Kingdom of God as they did.

Their initial response to the threats, intimidation, and persecution from their government officials was to pray. After they finished asking for a fresh infilling of boldness and courage to sweep through their community, God agreed with their prayer.

I promise you that embarking on a journey of bold prayers will put you in situations of hardship, trouble, and threats from the enemies of God. In other words, praying boldly will likely get you into some kind of trouble. Yet, the boldness available through it all will keep you on course and free you from the fear of consequences.

> After they prayed, the place where they were meeting was shaken. And they were all filled with the Holy Spirit and spoke the word of God boldly. (Acts 4:31)

Can you imagine being so in sync with what God is doing that this kind of supernatural encounter becomes normal? Yet that's what the Church of Acts experienced—and more! That is the ultimate goal of stepping into a new realm of bold prayers—to see God's transformational power released as He shows up in mightier and mightier ways.

We are living in unprecedented, fractured, intense times, and we need to respond in kind with unprecedented, unifying, intense prayers—bold prayers that ask according to the promises and prayers of Scripture. If we don't call Heaven down to Earth, who will? Who will be the intercessors that stand in the gap between right and wrong if not us?

Like those in the Book of Acts, we need to speak—and pray—the word of God boldly.

THREE

BOLD WORSHIP

The day after our Golden Gate Bridge experience, we traveled south to Huntington Beach in Orange County to worship and pray, and a thousand people showed up. It was amazing. Several people gave their lives to Jesus, and since the ocean was right there, we decided to baptize them on the spot. That Sunday, the *Los Angeles Times* ran an article under a headline that read, "In Huntington Beach, a revival with church at the ocean's edge." It was the most positive press we would see from a major news source for several months.

We went from there to New York City's Washington Square Park; well over a thousand people showed up, and spiritual fire began to burn on the East Coast. We returned to California the week after that, and almost five thousand people gathered on Cardiff State Beach in Encinitas near San Diego. We used the same battery-powered speaker we'd had on the Golden Gate Bridge, but the crowds were so large it was almost useless. Thankfully, it didn't hamper the atmosphere at all. Something beautiful was happening in the rawness and the stripping back. Our production (if that's what you want to call two tiny speakers and an acoustic guitar on a beach) was very underwhelming. Yet God's presence was there and felt by all who attended.

The next morning, which was a Monday, many pastors in the area were so emboldened that they approached county commissioners to reverse the church-closure order. As a result, the county made it legal for churches to gather in public spaces and parking lots.

We began to realize these gatherings were much more than just us and a lot of hungry people showing up. God was doing something significant. When that happens, you know you're going to face opposition.

If you gather a couple thousand people somewhere, it's going to get noticed and news sources are going to pick it up. There's no getting around that.

But as this happened, people started looking for ulterior motives in our movement, and reports about what we were doing started getting twisted. We began to see posts and articles saying we were gathering to defy the government and that we were right-wing COVID-deniers creating "superspreader" events. We were accused of hiding behind the First Amendment instead of practicing it. As awareness spread on social media and elsewhere, people started coming to protest our gatherings, chanting, "Put on a mask! Put on a mask!" even though we never discouraged any of the attendees from wearing masks. Some protestors even handed out or posted leaflets when we went into the streets of Los Angeles' Skid Row in late 2020 that read:

Resistance blockage against biological warfare
Protect the homeless, Sean Feucht, walk away!

They sent fifty cars to create a blockade to prevent us from passing out food to the homeless during our outreaches. Some even claimed everything we were doing was to stage photo ops so we could raise more money from our donors.

The truth, however, was that while we did want to show that we would not be silenced, our main motivation in continuing to hold the gatherings was because each time we did, God ministered to people who needed Him. We knew that people were in a tough place and needed God, and with most of the churches either closed or meeting online, there was little chance for them to receive the encouragement and healing they needed. As much as possible, we connected with churches in the cities where we held events so they could follow up with the people who attend our outreaches.

As much as we wish this weren't true, attending church online is just not the same as going in person, and the effects of the governor's edict were already showing. I have heard it said that online church could be compared to seeing and hearing a fire but not being able to feel its warmth. The Barna Group estimated that as many as one in three people stopped attending church all together because of the effects of the pandemic.[1]

During this time, while we were home in Redding, we did a Let Us Worship gathering that became very controversial—even among some our closest friends and church leaders. It really took us all by surprise. The Church is a diverse body and should be.

Jesus isn't into making carbon-copy Christians; He calls people from all walks of life, backgrounds, and perspectives. But even if we disagree on many things, we should always be able to find fellowship in our common pursuit of being more like Jesus.

I've always been able to openly discuss different political views with people without becoming offended—which I did a lot of during my run for Congress. I spoke with a lot of friends and acquaintances who saw things differently, but our relationships were first and foremost about the Kingdom of God. After all, I'm a musician and a worship leader, and most of us are the kind of people who just want to be liked. I would never purposely choose to create controversy or rock the boat; most of us just want to create an atmosphere where people can meet Jesus. Because of this, Kate and I have always had a solid base of friends and church family, even when we saw things differently than others.

This mandate by the governor, however, turned out to be different. It was a line drawn in the sand.

As more things were written about us, those closest to us began to question our motives along with the secular mainstream media. It was tough. I had a strong conviction that we needed to keep doing what we were doing and offer as many people as possible the answers only Jesus could provide. People were hurting, and we saw it firsthand when we went out to pray and worship all across America. In a lot of ways, it was the same thing we'd done in other places of the world, where the consequences were far more deadly than disobeying California's COVID restrictions.

But suddenly, it felt like everything was different. People who had always supported our overseas work started to question what we were doing. The COVID situation was more polarized than I had imagined. People even released statements reversing support of gatherings they had originally helped us organize or advertise.

It shook us—especially Kate. She and I have always been unified in all we do, and this was the first time we had a major disagreement about the direction of our ministry. In fact, when I still had my doubts about running for Congress, she was convinced I needed to do it. She insisted it was the right time for me to take a bold stand and run.

Now, she was convinced we'd crossed a line. It was too much for her.

"You have to stop this, Sean," she told me with tears in her eyes. "You're ruining our whole lives."

We were on our way from Redding to Pasadena, where we were going to do our next open-air event in a cul-de-sac next to a Hispanic church. Our kids were in the backseat, watching a movie. We'd already received three letters from the city of Los Angeles saying we would be arrested and taken to jail if we went forward with the event we had planned. So I had a lot of questions about it as well, but still felt like God was telling me to do it.

Kate disagreed—vehemently. It was so painful. It all gets very real when your own wife is against what you are doing.

I shook my head. I looked over at her and said, "I can't stop." I cared deeply about her feelings and did not want to continue with the events if it meant bringing division and distance between us. I was not ready to give up my family for some new form of ministry—but I felt strongly the fear of God on the idea that we had to continue.

When we got to the venue, she dropped me off and then went to her sister's house with the kids. She did not come to the event. She really wanted no part of it.

I just looked to Heaven and said, "God, I'll do this, but I can't go on without my wife or my family."

Again, God showed up in amazing ways as we lifted our voices in worship and prayer and ministered to the people in the crowd. It was incredible to see Him showing up in powerful encounters like the ones overseas in the streets of California.

I went home grateful for that night, but also thinking we had completed what God had called us to do. I didn't want to keep going with Let Us Worship if Kate didn't agree that we were being obedient to God.

As it turned out, maybe we were done in California for a while, but God had more for us to do across the nation that was now seeing racial protests, unrest, and calls for lawlessness.

The next week, I got a call from friends in Portland, Oregon. The city was going crazy. Violent protests over the George Floyd incident had been taking place almost every night since May, and it was now August. Rioters were burning copies of the Bible on the courthouse steps. The city had become an epicenter for Antifa-led violence, and they had all but taken over a downtown park. The images were flooding social media and dominating the news cycle.

I felt that, in the same way God had sent us into war zones across the world, we now needed to take His light into this area of darkness in our own nation.

We were once again being asked, "Will you answer My call?"

Unpredictable Praise

I had the most remarkable encounter with God when I was sixteen years old during my first trip to India. It forever transformed the way I view and engage in worship. Growing up in a comfortable, Western, contained, and predictable church culture, I needed the jolt and wildness of the nations to give me perspective on what really happens when we raise our voices in praise to God.

I had just begun learning to play guitar a few weeks before we left and could play a total of four chords! This allowed me to fumble my way through most worship songs. Simultaneously, the main worship leader in our youth group left for college, leaving a void. No one stepped up to fill his shoes, so the youth pastor asked me if I would take his place.

We had a fiery bunch of three hundred kids who met in a dingy primary school cafeteria every Wednesday night to pour out their hearts in worship to God. These nights were unrestrained and loud, and passion definitely prevailed over skill. The quality of the music probably wasn't pleasurable—okay, it was really horrible—but we were always full of zeal and authenticity. I cut my teeth in those early days of leading by ripping off versions of Delirous? worship songs from their *Cutting Edge* CD, adding my own tags, bridges, and choruses to spice things up.

I never had an ounce of desire to be a well-known worship leader, an artist on a major record label, or even produce my own albums one day. Instead, my dream from the very beginning was to use whatever simple skills I had to bring worship to the roughest and darkest places on Earth. I knew I would be content singing songs in a hut with a handful of people in a remote part of China somewhere. I wanted to follow in my parents' footsteps as a missionary to people who had never heard the Gospel. I figured that picking up the guitar would now make me a "musicianary."

That first day in northern India fulfilled many such dreams I held deep in my heart. The underground church movement was exploding there. Sikhs, Hindus, and Muslims were turning to Jesus in droves. Entire villages were getting saved, putting India on track to surpass China as having the fastest-growing underground church in the world. Despite intense opposition and persecution, the church was thriving, and the setting for most gatherings was usually in the backyard or on the farmland of the latest convert.

After landing in Delhi in the summer of 2000, we took an overnight train north. After getting a quick three hours of sleep, a local pastor in a "rickshaw" (what they call a three-wheeled bicycle taxi) picked me up. The pastor had planted more than ten thousand churches across the region, and yet he was one of the humblest men I had ever met. He told me we had a full day of church meetings in several different villages ahead of us. I rubbed my eyes and nodded eagerly.

On our way to the first of three Sunday morning services where I'd been asked to sing and share, the pastor received a frantic call. The man on the other end of the line begged us to stop by his home immediately. He told us his wife was possessed by a demonic spirit and was destroying their house. She was running around with knives, threatening to sacrifice their children on an altar she built the previous night in their backyard.

Hello newbie missionary—welcome to India!

Without much explanation, the pastor shouted to the taxi driver to take a sharp left, and we made our way down a winding dirt road to the man's house. When we stepped inside, we were greeted with screams, moans, and the sounds of dishes being shattered and furniture being destroyed. The pastor told me to crouch in a corner of the house away from harm. With a smile on his face, he told me this would only take a few minutes and then we would be on our way. He acted like he was completely in control the entire time! I was in the absolute opposite state of mind. I was shocked, alarmed, and pretty rattled.

I had never in my life seen anything like this. This little four-and-a-half-foot-tall Indian woman had eyes that were bright red, and she was screaming in a deep manly voice. It was like a scene out of a horror movie. I had never imagined I would see anything like this in my entire life.

With wide eyes, I watched the pastor take out a small, beaten-up tambourine from his dusty backpack. He began to worship and pray in the midst of the chaos, fear, and confusion filling that house. It was like he was grasping a well-worn worship weapon. The tambourine only had about half of its dangly little bronze cymbals left, as far as I could tell.

After a few minutes of rattling his tambourine and filling the kitchen with song, the woman crumpled to the ground and began weeping. I witnessed the transformation of total deliverance as the pastor walked around, continuing to sing and pray.

After feeling an atmosphere of peace finally settle in, he walked over to the transformed woman and hugged her while her family rushed in from wherever they had been hiding. They embraced their mother and each other in tears as they celebrated the deliverance. The horror and screaming was replaced with worship. Never have I felt an atmosphere shift so quickly and completely!

After a while longer, we prayed again together, thanking God for His freedom descending in this home. We declared that the evil spirits would never return. As we walked out the door back to the rickshaw, the pastor looked at me and smiled. "Don't you see, Sean? When we worship with boldness and courage, the demons will always flee!"

This short encounter would forever mark my life. It would teach me more than any books I read, courses I was taught in college, or sermons I heard in church. The experience I had with that illiterate, uneducated, underground pastor in rural India will stay with me for the rest of my life.

The wild thing is that this experience is not unique to the pastors in northern India, or to those in many other parts of the world. This is part of their everyday lives. They do not view worship as a trendy fad consisting of three fast songs, three slow songs, a light show, a smoke machine, and brooding music led by hipster-looking kids with perfect hair, skinny jeans, and tattoos. The remote places of the world can't turn on a local K-LOVE station to encourage them as they cruise in their minivan to the local mall. In most developing nations, worship is their lifeline amidst very real persecution and oppression. *Bold worship* is the only kind of worship they know—worship that flies in the face of fear, opposition, demonic possession, threats, and intimidation. It's something they need every single day they wake up.

Bold worship never allows circumstances to steal our song. Bold worship is like fervent prayer. It is like the army marching tirelessly around the tall fortress of Jericho, preparing to blast trumpets on the conclusion of the seventh lap. (See Joshua 5:13–6:27.) It shouts and declares God's faithfulness in the face of enemy fortifications. It forces the walls of the enemy to absorb the roar of victory before the victory becomes a reality.

This is the same worship Paul and Silas tapped into when imprisoned and facing certain death in Philippi. (See Acts 16:16–40.) Their bold midnight worship did not just bring them freedom, but opened up every single prison door around them.

King Jehoshaphat also tapped into bold worship when he called the nation of Judah to rise up and praise in its darkest hour. (See 2 Chronicles 20.) The nation was surrounded by an army so vast and intimidating that its end could not be seen, so he commanded everyone to *"sing to the Lord for the splendor of his holiness!"* (2 Chronicles 20:21). This seemed silly, reckless, and more than just a little delusional. Yet as Scripture records, it was the key to Judah's victory.

> As they began to sing and praise, the Lord set ambushes against the men of Ammon and Moab and Mount Seir who were invading Judah, and they were defeated. (2 Chronicles 20:22)

All these historical and biblical situations followed the identical scenario:

> *You see that big issue in front of you that feels hopeless, discouraging, and life-threatening? Go ahead and ignore it! Go ahead and sing over it! There is a breakthrough*

coming on the other end of your song! Focus on the One who is above it all and anchor your hope in what Heaven declares!

This response is brazen. It is bold. It is fearless. And it is biblical.

Our worship should not get quieter or more subdued during times of trial, uncertainty, or darkness—it should get louder and more explosive than ever before!

The war zones and persecution hot spots around the world have been the places that most formed the worship expression inside of me over the past twenty years. Though I have been fortunate to be an artist on a successful record label and have written songs with some of the most esteemed Christian artists on earth, it is the persecuted churches of Iraq, India, China, and North Korea that formed the bold sound inside me. Every time these precious saints gather to worship God, it truly is a sacrifice of praise because they risk everything they have when they do it. Many of those nameless and faceless leaders have sacrificed their reputations, been forever ostracized from family, and been blacklisted from future jobs. Every time they open their mouths in worship, they face possible imprisonment, torture, and death for their refusal to be silent. And yet silent they are not.

We must understand the very real battle raging every morning when we wake up and open our eyes. We are in a constant battle over who will be worshipped on the earth. This was what Jesus Himself faced when He was tempted by the devil in the wilderness:

Again, the devil took him to a very high mountain and showed him all the kingdoms of the world and their splendor. "All this I will give you," he said, "if you will bow down and worship me." (Matthew 4:8)

If the Son of God faced such opposition and temptation, why would we think our journey in life would be any different? Many times, the layers of resistance we face to worship with boldness and courage prove how scared the enemy is of the sound of our praise. This is why we cannot back down. We cannot live in fear and silence. Bold worship creates pockets of the Kingdom of God on Earth where His will is done just as it is in Heaven.

Bold worship is the sound we need filling our homes when heaviness creeps in. Bold worship is what we need to release when we experience pain, trauma, opposition, or conflict. The very thing the enemy tries to silence is the very thing that can and will bring our greatest breakthrough!

Today, do not hold back in expressing your worship and love to Jesus. Let the sound be released, and do not stop until you see the walls crash down, the prison doors open, and the freedom of God manifest in your life!

Praise the Lord!

FOUR

BOLD MISSIONS

*Whoever wants to be my disciple must deny themselves
and take up their cross daily and follow me.*

—Luke 9:23

After L.A., we had Let Us Worship gatherings in Redding, Bakersfield, Fresno, then in San Diego—and that was the one that really turned the tide for Kate. It was not that she did not like worship, prayer, outreach, or any of the stuff we had been giving our lives to since we had been married; it was more that she was just tired of everything in our lives being a fight since the congressional run. It was hard to see the purpose of it all. Why should we enter another battle so quickly when we were still not healed up from the last one? But that moment of purpose came to her on Cardiff State Beach when our seven-year-old son, Ezra, asked to be baptized.

He had wanted to be baptized for a while by that point, but with churches closed, we never knew when that might happen. So on the beach there in San Diego, when we asked if people wanted to be baptized, he came to me and said, "Dad, I want to get baptized tonight." It happened at the very end of the meeting with hundreds of others who braved the cold waters of the Pacific to make a public declaration of their faith. The video of my son's baptism was aired on Fox News and other networks across America the next morning. For a brief moment in a rather tumultuous 2020, America began to see some signs of hope and new life.

I don't think I recognized it completely at the time, but it was a powerful moment for our family. It just brought everything into a different light, and it became undeniable that God was behind what was happening in each city we worshipped and prayed in.

At the same time, Kate came to terms with the cost of moving forward and taking these revival meetings outside of California—where there was opposition enough—and into the heart of cities that were going crazy with protests, and even riots, like Portland, Seattle, and New York. It wasn't the danger that bothered her so much as the relationships it looked like this journey would cost us. Our nice, safe little life in Northern California of being "the crazy missionary worship leader who ran for Congress" would be gone forever. We were going to lose friends, and all kinds of things would be said about us behind our backs and online. The media would attack us. The whole narrative of who we were would be distorted.

And we were never going to be able to go back to our previous reality. We had to let it go. This was the hard part. We had finally found an amazing and somewhat predictable life for our family. After living in four different cities in four states over fifteen years of marriage, raising four babies, and traveling to more than fifty nations as a family, we finally felt like we had found our home, rhythm, and community in a quaint Northern California town. It felt like we were about to settle down for the long haul for the very first time in our crazy family journey.

We lived on a country property with a home, a barn, and fifteen acres, and we'd found a groove that worked. I was a part of a well-known Christian record label, we loved our home church, our kids loved their school, and life was good. Since the accidental launch of Let Us Worship on the Golden Gate Bridge that day and the controversy that ensued (at home and abroad), like a snow globe at Christmas, God was shaking up our perfect little life and all that we held dear. We had to choose between following the move of God or going back—and if we followed the move, going back would never be an option again. It was a tough follow-up to what had happened during the congressional run, but that's just how it went. We had to be willing for it to cost us everything to keep chasing after what God was putting on our hearts to do.

And we decided we were.

Answering When He Calls

The mandate of the Great Commission is simply to bring the message of God's hope and salvation everywhere we go.

> Then Jesus came to them and said, "All authority in heaven and on earth has been given to me. Therefore go and make disciples of all nations, baptizing them in the name of the Father and of the Son and of the Holy Spirit, and teaching them to obey everything I have commanded you. And surely I am with you always, to the very end of the age." (Matthew 28:18–20)

This mandate for missions does not just apply to those giving their lives to reach some unreached people group. This is for every single believer! Our neighborhoods, businesses, supermarkets, and schools are filled with lost souls looking for hope, life, and a purpose.

Without the impartation of boldness to share the Good News, there can be no fulfillment of the Great Commission. Courage and boldness are the keys! If we don't take the Gospel into dark places, who will?

My parents gave up everything to answer this call. My dad had worked hard to build a thriving medical practice in Missoula, Montana, when I was growing up, but then went on a mission trip to Romania that changed him for life. Not many years later, he left everything to chase the calling full-time he had first felt on that trip. As far as I know, he never considered it a sacrifice.

The news of the sudden sale of his medical practice shocked our little town so much that the newspaper ran a front-page article on it. In like fashion, my mom, a registered nurse, quit her job at the hospital to lead teams overseas bringing the hope, love, and healing of Jesus. My three sisters and I grew up with a strong culture that joyfully forsook many of the pleasures, luxuries, and successes of the world to run after "the least of these" and the unreached people groups in nations far away. Instead of buying boats, second homes, and recreational toys, my parents spent their extra money on trips to the nations. Many times, they took us along for the ride.

My dad carried a soft spot for the hard-to-get-to places around the world. He loved to bring hope, healing, and the message of salvation to places like Nepal, where the Tibetan Buddhists were living in deeply isolated mountain villages. He was thrown in prison in North Korea during his first trip there in the late 1990s. My parents also loved the remote corners of the Amazonian jungles of Brazil. My dad was part of the first foreign missions team on the ground in January 2005 when a tsunami wiped out Banda Aceh in Indonesia and 227,000 souls perished across the islands. Though a quiet, patient, and kind man, his steady boldness was evident by the fruit of his life. He pushed the envelope of what boldness on the mission field truly looks like.

I saw this firsthand in the Amazonian jungles when my dad took me on my first mission trip when I was twelve. More than fifteen doctors and medical personnel boarded a small boat outside the city of Manaus, and we traveled as far as the river would allow to reach some of the most isolated people on earth. Some of the languages were so obscure that we would need two or even three interpreters to find the correct dialect in order to communicate as we set up medical clinics on the banks of the river.

I watched the doctors, nurses, and dentists work from dawn until dusk every day praying, diagnosing, and treating diseases they had never seen in a textbook. I watched demons manifest, people get delivered, and the lame begin to walk. I saw miracles break out so strongly no one could deny that the power of God was *real!*

After a full day's work, we would thank God for all He had done. Then we would clean up by jumping in the river for a quick bath, board the boat as the sun was setting, and set sail for another village. It was grueling, yet still some of the most satisfying and powerful work I have ever been a part of.

I was baptized for the first time on the last day of that trip as black piranhas and every creepy creature of the Amazon swam below me. I knew coming up out of the water that my destiny was in the nations. That encounter in the jungles of Brazil forever shaped what missions would look like for me. I was determined to go where the Gospel was needed most.

The current shaking, shifting, and turmoil among the nations has created an insatiable hunger for people to truly discover the purpose of their existence. Collectively, the patterns of our lives have been disrupted in a once-in-a-generation way. The pandemic has shaken the predictability off our lives and exposed our vulnerabilities and false securities, and collectively, we have found ourselves to be far more vulnerable and fragile than we ever imagined. Our individual worlds became volatile and unpredictable in a matter of days. We discovered we were not as in control of this life as we once thought. This season has also exposed the faultiness of what we were building our lives upon. We discovered that our foundations were untrustworthy. And just when we wanted to go out and find answers, we all got locked inside.

Romans 8:19 and 22 tells us

> Creation waits in eager expectation for the children of God to be revealed.... The whole creation has been groaning as in the pains of childbirth right up to the present time.

There is a deep longing inside the earth for truth and justice. There is a shaking and sifting to determine what is real and what is eternal. The earth groans for its Creator and His appointed guardians to take their proper places in leadership and stewardship. Never has the world been riper to hear the message of true redemption only found in the person of Jesus Christ. Never have so many been leaning in to hear bold witnesses declare the hope of new life, salvation, and the Solid Rock to stand upon.

During my high school years in Chesapeake, Virginia, we were part of a very missional church. My dad became the missions pastor, and we sent more than twenty-five missions teams per year to virtually every continent on earth. In addition, teams were sent to New York City and an Indian reservation in Montana to conduct outreach and kids' camps and bring the love of Jesus to various communities. It was normal for kids in my youth group to go on one of these trips every summer. In fact, one summer, Kate went on a trip that my mom led to Italy, and I went on one with her dad to St. Lucia in the Caribbean.

Back home sitting in the cafeteria of our high school one day, I got to thinking. *Why do we always wait until we are overseas to do "missions work"? Why isn't it just second nature to do it where we are? Do we not want the people we see every day to know what we believe? We travel to exotic locations to share our deepest beliefs there instead. Why are we different "at home"?*

Convicted that I was being hypocritical, I launched a campaign from our house called "Take the Neighborhood for Jesus." It consisted of my youth group members meeting at our house on Saturday morning and doing door-to-door witnessing for most of that day (with a small break for lunch). We started with a pep talk and a prayer together. We shared testimonies highlighting the breakthroughs that happened the week before and how God moved. Then we discussed different evangelism strategies and ideas for how we could better connect with our neighbors. We loved to pray for people, share the love of Jesus, and practice our "bold witness."

At the time, Chesapeake was rated as one of the safest cities in the nation and one of the best places to raise a family. It was prototypical, classic American suburbia where kids rode their bikes everywhere and no one worried where you were until it started getting dark. How could we be bold overseas in remote places closed to the Gospel if we couldn't have a bold witness in the safety of our neighborhoods?

I thought taking our bold witness to the streets of Chesapeake would be a great idea and the neighbors would all love it! While lots of them did, a few were adamantly opposed, even though very few refused to let us pray for them. Even those who were atheist, agnostic, or of another religion were happy for us to pray over their homes, families, and businesses. I saw it as a hunger rising up for a touch from God.

The few who were adamantly opposed, though, were very vocal. They raised the issue at a homeowners' association meeting, and we were eventually barred from evangelizing door-to-door in the three major subdivisions surrounding my house. But by that time, we had reached hundreds of homes and seen radical salvations, healings, and miracles (and even enjoyed some delicious free meals along the way).

One man who was touched was an old Vietnam veteran who lived on a corner lot. His lawn was always meticulously mowed and bright green. His vintage Ford Mustang was perfectly waxed and shiny, always catching your eye from where it was parked in his driveway. His American flag always waved gently in the breeze and never seemed to get tangled up. All the same, he was someone I felt the Holy Spirit say needed true freedom.

One day when we went to his door, he approached us on the sidewalk and asked us (using some rather choice profanity) what we were doing. I explained that we were going door to door, sharing the love of Jesus with the neighborhood. He exploded. "Don't you kids read the signs in the neighborhood and in my yard? *There is no soliciting here!*"

I politely explained that we were not coming to sell anything but simply to pray for whoever wanted a touch from God. He sharply quipped back, "*See!* Right there! You are selling *Jesus*! *No soliciting!*"

"No," I countered, "we are not. He's a free gift and you can receive Him right now if you'd like!"

He threw his hands up in the air. "Get off my sidewalk and away from my property!"

We respected his wishes and moved on.

Despite this rough beginning, week after week, we wore him down with our kindness. I think, being a military guy, he just couldn't resist our tenacity.

Finally, one day he asked me, "Why do you all keep coming back time and time again?"

I explained that we loved him, Jesus loved him, and we were there anytime he needed prayer or encouragement. We just wanted to keep checking back so we could be there when he did.

The highlight of that whole season was the one time I got to pray for him. Great emotion came over him as we honored his sacrifice for our country and prayed that God would heal the pain and trauma he had experienced from being at war.

God taught us something important in all of that. He never intends for people to be "salvation projects." We don't share the

Gospel for some kind of tally kept somewhere in Heaven for us to garner favor with God. We are to sow the seeds of the Gospel out of what we experience with Him. Sharing is one way we overcome ourselves to better let Jesus show through us. With every person my group got the privilege of praying for, our hearts grew bolder and our faith for God to move increased. There is no heart too hard for love the of God to penetrate, regardless of whether it belongs to a diehard Sikh in the tribes of northern India or the veteran down the block.

This revelation eventually led to me heading for Iraq with my family years later in the wake of the ISIS attacks there. I'll never forget that day—August 19, 2014. I was about to take off from Dulles International Airport in Washington, D.C., for London for the launch of Hillside, our brand-new worship and missions training school in the United Kingdom. I was getting situated in my seat for the long flight when I checked my phone one last time before putting it in airplane mode. As I scrolled through Twitter, my fingers accidentally hit a link to a video that popped up on my screen and began to play.

The video was of ISIS terrorists beheading journalist James Foley. Before I could even exit out of the video, I had seen the entire thing. It was an image I knew I could never unsee.

A righteous rage grew in me that kept me awake the entire red-eye flight to London. *How is it even possible that something this barbaric and demonic could happen in our day for everyone to see?* The level of fear and panic that was being broadcast to the world in that moment was unbelievable.

Although multiple platforms scrambled to take the video down, it spread like a wildfire across the internet. It was the coming-out party for ISIS, and the whole world was watching.

When I landed in London, I was scheduled to deliver an inaugural speech to open the training session at our school. But what was supposed to be a rather jovial and lighthearted address turned into a call to arms laced with an urgency I had not known before. I shared about David and Goliath and how our smooth stones of worship have to slay the giants of fear and darkness in the land. I ended by spontaneously announcing that we were going to send a team into the heart of Iraq and raise up a courageous band of worshippers who were not afraid to give their lives for Jesus. I admitted that I did not know how we were going to do it or even when it would happen, but I knew our mandate as a school and movement was not to create famous worship leaders. The world needed presence-carriers, not performers—those who could release the sound of Heaven to change the atmosphere and bring God's Kingdom into these places.

When I returned home, I began looking for a team willing to go into the ISIS-infested heart of Iraq from which so many Christians and missionaries were then fleeing. Within a month of the viral beheading video, almost every major missions organization I knew pulled their missionaries from the Iraq-Syria war zone and sent them home. How was I going to recruit fresh, optimistic, courageous missionaries to the very place everyone else was running from? Where would I find the people equipped with the boldness, tenacity, and—as some would later call it, *insanity*—to do this?

I wanted to be one of the first to respond and go myself. That is how excited I was about the situation. But after extensive talks with my wife, we agreed this was not the time for our family to be there. We had two toddlers and a brand-new baby at home. So I started calling every crazy, missionally minded person I knew. No one seemed to feel called to go. No one felt the same urgency. No one saw the opportunity I did, either.

Then one night as I was returning home from a date with Kate, I started talking to our babysitter about Iraq. I was carrying this burden pretty heavily, so I seemed to discuss the need with whoever would listen. For some reason, I felt led to open up to her specifically about how amazingly open the door is for the Gospel in the midst of trauma and chaos. She was intrigued and began to ask me questions, one after another. It turned out she had always dreamed of living in the Middle East and serving refugees with the love of God.

One thing led to another, and a few weeks later she determined that she was going to be the first to commit to moving to Iraq! I could hardly believe it. This was far from what I had in mind when I first pitched the vision in London during our worship school: a twenty-something, blonde-haired, single white woman was the last person I ever would have chosen to send to that part of the world, yet she was the first one to say yes.

We quickly began working together to raise her support, recruit more people to join her, and do our best to prepare her for all the unknowns she would face. It just so happened that two of her friends also felt led to move to Iraq, and they were also young women who had babysat our kids from time to time. Suddenly our launch team had grown to three willing people—and they were all our babysitters! They all fulfilled their three-year commitments on the ground and pioneered some amazing work there that continues today.

I have heard it said that God does not call the qualified, but qualifies the called. These women were young, optimistic, very green, and "unqualified" according to many, yet they were the first to answer God's call to go to some of the neediest people in the world. They established our first Light A Candle missions base in the middle of a war zone. Many more would later follow their "Yes," but it took a few bold hearts to pave the way.

No Christian is exempt from the call of Jesus to take the Gospel to the ends of the earth. You may not feel called to go to North Korea, Afghanistan, or Iraq like we have in recent years, but your neighbor next door and your coworkers all need Jesus just as much as those in the farthest and darkest nations. My encouragement to you is this: *Do not wait!*

Let us make haste and burn with passion, fire, and boldness for the lost! It is our calling and mission today more than ever. People are gripped with fear and trapped in darkness, but we can bring them the light. Today is the day to answer that call.

FIVE

BOLD LEADERSHIP

*Courage is contagious. When a brave man takes a
stand, the spines of others are often stiffened.*

—Billy Graham

After Kate and I came into agreement on going to Portland,
we started planning for it. Almost as soon as we sent out our
first emails to our newsletter list and announced it on social media,
pastors began sending responses questioning what we were planning. Though every message was different, all of them were essentially asking us, "Why would you invite our people to worship in
the most dangerous place in the city—one of the most dangerous
places in America?"

Somehow, "because that's what we do all over the world"
wasn't an acceptable answer. Somehow doing what we do overseas
in our own backyards was a completely different—and incredibly
insensitive—thing to do.

The rioting had been going in Portland for more than 100 days
in a row. Every major news outlet was covering the violence, and
night after night, fear, division, and hopelessness were being

broadcast across America from the exact place we were going to hold our gathering. It had become the symbol of everything wrong with our nation. The local government and police failed to enforce basic safety for the citizenry; meanwhile, Antifa and affiliated groups were claiming that Portland was *their* city and they could do whatever they wanted in it.

We were soon fighting opposition on all sides. All of our requests for permits to hold a public event were denied. Despite the fact that protestors had been gathering in the streets of Portland for months to scream profanity, threaten innocent citizens, damage property, burn buildings, and harass police officers, we couldn't get support from the local government to hold a peaceful and unifying worship gathering at a time the city desperately needed it.

Not only that, but we also couldn't find any worship leaders, musicians, sound guys, or anyone else who would help us set up, run production elements, or be on the stage with us representing their city. It was crazy. We'd never had anything like that happen before in any city we had been to so far. There was always an immediate buy-in from many local people. Since it was about their city, not us being there, it seemed hard to justify going in when no one was brave enough to join us.

A few days before the event, however, a leader called me from a local Slavic church. "We heard you want to come to Portland and worship and pray in the park downtown. We are with you and believe this is the call of God on us, too. How can we help?"

I was floored. The man offered us help setting up and tearing down, musicians, the use of the church's sound equipment, and someone to run it all for us. He even said he had a group that would help with security. It was an absolute answer to prayer and a godsend to us! But most importantly, it brought confirmation that we were really supposed to hold the event in Portland.

I had to ask him, "Why would you guys do this? Why are you willing to do it when on one else is?"

"We refuse to let our city become like the cities we left in Russia," he told me over the phone. "We had to leave Russia because the government used any and every excuse to try to keep us silent. We cannot let the same thing happen here."

The day before the event, the chaplain for the local police department called me out of the blue to let me know there wouldn't be any police protection for us because law enforcement had too many other higher-priority things going on. He personally believed in all we were doing. He confided that one of the things his men were facing was a teenage street gang going around randomly stabbing people. The deputies were working to apprehend the members of this gang, in addition to many other facets of the crime wave sweeping across the city. According to the FBI, homicides in Portland rose 82.8 percent in 2020 compared to 2019.[1] The streets were completely out of control, and the police were not effective at stopping things. They were at the end of their ropes and their resources were depleted.

"Sean, I know you have a constitutional right to do this, but I'm asking you as a fellow believer who loves the Lord, please don't," he said. "We can't protect you. We can't control what happens down there. I'm worried for your safety and the safety of anyone who attends. If you do this, you're responsible for everyone there. If someone gets hurt, their blood will be on *your* hands. You need to feel the weight of that."

And by the time we got off the phone, I did. A heaviness came over me. Thoughts began to attack my mind. *Who do you think you are, anyway? What do you think you're going to accomplish by doing this? Why would you endanger people's lives? Something bad is going to happen, and it will be your fault! You're just being arrogant, and you are going to get people hurt for no reason other than your ego.*

It was the morning of the event, and we were staying on a friend's farm outside Portland. I began wondering again if we should pull the plug. I decided to go for a jog and pray about it.

Partway into the jog, a peace settled over me. I felt the Lord impress on me, *I've called you to do this. You need to listen to My voice.*

We were on. God was with us. We were going to go into the darkest place in the city and lift up the name of the Lord, even if it was just a few of us.

Between five thousand and seven thousand people showed up that night. There had been no marketing, no boosted ads, everybody against us, and yet Christians still turned out in droves. The sight of it was staggering—it was an *army!* A black pastor showed up with his entire choir, and they opened worship with us.

It was one of the most powerful moments I've ever been part of. We could see the desperation of the people calling out to God. While there were some who showed up because they wanted to defy the government and did not care about worship, they quickly found out a few minutes into the event that's not what we were about.

We were going to go after revival, and we preached the Gospel. We preached against fear. People got saved. People got delivered of anxiety and depression. Black pastors ministered to angry white protesters. The park is right on the Willamette River, so we ended the night with baptisms—and there were so many wanting to be baptized, we had to do them two or three at a time. It was iconic. Again, God showed up in a tremendous way.

Imagine the surprise of all who had opposed us when thousands of bold and courageous believers from across the Pacific Northwest resisted the narratives of fear and intimidation and showed up to worship God in Waterfront Park. The clips of our Let Us Worship gathering in Portland went viral across social media and national news outlets in the days following. The very spot where darkness seems so pervasive was transformed into a beacon of hope for many.

The next morning, I was doing interviews with major media outlets when God surprised us yet again with another miracle. Up until that point, we had not had very many spiritual leaders with national platforms backing us. I'm sure it seemed like this was a rogue movement to many. Since our home church in Redding, California, was still closed for regular services, the fact that we were doing something so radically different created friction in some people's minds. Many pastors and leaders wanted to know what spiritual covering we had as we held these large gatherings across America. However, Franklin Graham (son of the great evangelist Billy Graham), wrote something on social media that ended up as the most shared post in America that day:

> There was some good news from this weekend. I don't know Sean Feucht, but I love what he's doing! He's going right into the places that have some of the worst rioting and leading worship services outdoors. He's not afraid. He knows Jesus Christ is the only answer for the human

heart—and people are surrendering their lives to Christ! Thousands gathered this weekend in Portland and Seattle. God bless him!

Sean has been hosting Let Us Worship "protests" across California to encourage Christians to become more involved in politics and fight against the "double standard" seen in coronavirus restrictions. The targeting of churches by government officials to limit or ban attendance is an indication of what's at stake in this country in the next election. It's immensely important that we make this a matter of prayer and vote for leadership who stand with the Constitution and defend our religious freedoms.

That was the first time I realized we had been given a grace to go into these difficult cities in our own nation. Just as God had called us to go into Iraq, North Korea, and Afghanistan, He was calling us to go into the areas of protest, pain, and riots in the United States to shine forth His light and hope. While there were edicts against these gatherings from governments, threats from protest groups, and a hellish target painted on many of these events, we sensed a very different mandate from Heaven. We had to keep pushing into it.

It Starts with One Person

All through the Bible, when things seemed the darkest, God would anoint a man or woman to lead the way and bring forth His light. We see it when He called Moses to go back to Egypt to set His people free; we see it all through the Book of Judges when He raised up leaders like Deborah, Gideon, and Samson; and we see it when Israel entered the Promised Land under the leadership of Joshua after Moses's death. In each of these situations, things seemed hopeless, but God stepped in to fill His people with faith.

For me, the words of the first chapter of Joshua ring as true today as when they were first spoken millennia ago.

In commissioning Joshua to lead His people, God stated bluntly: "Moses my servant is dead." (Joshua 1:2)

When we talk about leadership, it's easy to look to the past for great leaders we wish were still with us to take us through the hard times we're experiencing now. In essence, though, what God was saying in that statement was, "There's no going back. The time of Moses's leadership has passed. If you are going to take my people into the land I have promised them, it's going to be up to you."

I think we're in a similar time as Christians right now. Many of our greatest leaders of the past are gone. Billy Graham, Reinhard Bonnke, Luis Palau, and others who led huge crusades and gathered tens or even hundreds of thousands when they spoke have all gone the way of Moses. They're not here anymore. Therefore, it is up to our generation to step into the leadership vacuum they've left and see God's will done on Earth as it is in Heaven.

God went on from there:

> Now then, you and all these people, get ready to cross the Jordan River into the land I am about to give to them—to the Israelites. I will give you every place where you set your foot, as I promised Moses. (Joshua 1:2–3)

Note that in order for God's people to claim the land, He didn't say, "Pray that you be given the land," or "Ask Me to move the corrupt people from your path so you may enter in," or anything of the kind. Instead, He said, "Go there. Cross the river. Be in that place. Place the soles of your feet into the footprints of those who oppose you. Be salt and light in the places where I have been forgotten. Then I can give you those places just as I promised I would."

> No one will be able to stand against you all the days of your life. As I was with Moses, so I will be with you; I will never leave you nor forsake you. Be strong and courageous, because you will lead these people to inherit the land I swore to their ancestors to give them. Be strong and very courageous. (Joshua 1:5–7a)

To make sure they get it, God twice tells them: "Be strong and courageous." God was essentially saying, "I know my part. My part is to back you up and fill you with light so you can be a light in dark places. When you show up, I will show up, but I can't show up if you don't go into the darkness first. If you are afraid and stay home, you can't take Me there. You have to boldly go first."

Then God gives a condition:

> Be careful to obey all the law my servant Moses gave you; do not turn from it to the right or to the left, that you may be successful wherever you go. Keep this Book of the Law always on your lips; meditate on it day and night, so that you may be careful to do everything

written in it. Then you will be prosperous and successful. (Joshua 1:7–8)

God is saying here that when we go, we must do things His
way and hold up His values and words. As we are told in 2 Corinthians 5:20: "*We are therefore Christ's ambassadors, as though
God were making his appeal through us. We implore you on
Christ's behalf: Be reconciled to God.*" It's about His Gospel and
letting Him touch and deliver those who turn to Him. Again, we
go, and He shows up.

Then God concludes by encouraging Joshua a third time to act
with courage:

Have I not commanded you? Be strong and courageous.
Do not be afraid; do not be discouraged, for the Lord
your God will be with you wherever you go. (Joshua
1:9)

Before we showed up in Portland, the Pacific Northwest really
felt desperate. Portland was setting records for continual protests
and rioting, and in Seattle, protestors had actually cordoned off a
section of downtown with barriers and told the police they weren't
welcome in it. It's not something we're used to seeing here in the
States, though it epitomized a lot of what has been happening in
other nations around the world where lawless groups seek to over-
turn regional authority, or governments try to shut out God by
using any law or loophole they can. As someone once said during
the chaos and violence of the French Revolution: "The only thing

necessary for the triumph of evil is for good men [and women] to do nothing."

In contrast to that, however, I like the words of Billy Graham from the beginning of this chapter: "Courage is contagious. When a brave man [or woman] takes a stand, the spines of others are often stiffened." This is exactly what happened when thousands showed up to declare "Jesus is Lord" in Waterfront Park. People across the nation—and throughout the nations—got a chance to see a narrative of hope rather than one of despair.

Before our event, I wasn't sure if there were five hundred Christians willing to attend, let alone five to seven thousand that were unwilling to be intimidated by Antifa or anarchists, violence, or the lack of police protection. These courageous people did not allow fear or a need to protect themselves from harm to trump the call of God to bring hope to their city.

I have to admit, to be part of making that happen was pretty cool.

What happened in Portland, though, wasn't easy. We faced a lot of opposition and questioned what we were doing every step of the way. Honestly, going in, we had no idea what was going to happen. We even had serious reasons to believe someone was going to get hurt. (In fact, Kate was all but assaulted on her way to the park for the event.) No one would have objected to us backing out. Many would have even considered us wise for doing so. They probably even would have praised us.

But how different would things be in that city and across our nation now if we had backed down? Had we not placed our feet into rioters' footsteps, speaking blessings where they cursed, who knows how much worse things might be there now.

The event became a flash point of unity. Almost before we left, churches began to open again all over the region, and a spirit of unity grew as they did. For them, it must've been similar to the Israelites taking that first step into the Jordan to cross over into the Promised Land. As Joshua and other leaders took the first step, others became willing. Courage is contagious.

It's often easy to look back into the past and see that God's promises are real. It also seems easy to look overseas into dark and distant lands and feel like it just makes sense that God will show up in those places in miraculous ways. *But now? In* this *place? For me? In my own backyard?* We often act like trusting in God's promises closer to home is audacious at best, and completely foolhardy and reckless at worst.

I want to note as well that Joshua wasn't instructed to be unrealistic about what the Israelites were facing. God didn't say the armies of Canaan weren't formidable, or that the giants in the land weren't real. For us, COVID was very real, and the rioting and violence of the protestors was very real. In fact, we were confronted by them from the very minute we started setting up. We were vigilant all the way through to be sure they didn't damage our equipment or our event. We took precautions. It was just that we refused to let any of it stop us from doing what we felt God was telling us to do.

And, oddly enough, the fact that things turned out well doesn't mean we were right about that. Even if we had been hurt or something else had happened to stop us, that wouldn't have meant God wasn't with us or that we were somehow special. It's good to keep in mind that thousands of people around the world are thrown in prison, beaten, or even lose their lives every day because they are obedient witnesses for Jesus. (Just read a couple stories in a book I read again and again growing up, *Jesus Freaks* by dc Talk and the Voice of the Martyrs, and you'll see. God doesn't promise that we'll always succeed, but we are promised that standing up for Jesus will make a difference.)

We just had to have the conviction that God's promises were more real than the world's threats. When we showed up in Portland, we were declaring, "Hey, listen, God's promises are still here. They're still accessible to us today. They are still ours if we'll just cross over and take the land. We just need to take the next step."

In many ways, it comes down to the crux of what inspired me to write this book in the first place. Boldness is not motivated by fear, but by a deep conviction that some "realities" aren't negotiable. In our decision-making, which weighs on us more: what God says or what society says? In our vision and the path we pave as leaders—even if we are just leading ourselves—is our first thought, "What would God think of me doing that?" or is it, "I'd better not, because I might offend somebody"?

The Bible tells us that "the fear of the Lord is the beginning of wisdom" (Psalm 111:10; Proverbs 9:10). I don't think this is because God wants us to be afraid of Him in the traditional sense. I think it's because fear is a basic motivator of action, and quite often, when we need to make a decision, fear will tip the scale faster than logic or reason. If we fear what others think of us or that something we do might offend someone, then the kneejerk reaction is not to do that thing.

However, what if our immediate reaction were, "What would God think if I did (or didn't) do this?" Like, "What would God think if I didn't offer love in this situation?" or "What would God think if I skipped out on this opportunity to praise Him?" or "What would God think if I valued the opinions of my friends more than what the Bible says?"

If we did that, I think we would act—and lead—very differently than we do. And I think that is what the Bible means when it says the fear of the Lord is the *beginning* of wisdom, not the end; it's that place of obedience that makes bold leadership possible.

God's not done yet. He hasn't abandoned us. Before the end of things, He's going to make at least one more push for the hearts of our own nations. If we're going to be part of that, we have to be strong and very courageous. We have to be bold. That's what Joshua did in his season and what I believe God wants us to do in ours. It is still time to take the land for Jesus.

SIX

BOLD LOVE

For in Christ, neither our most conscientious religion
nor disregard of religion amounts to anything.
What matters is something far more interior:
faith expressed in love.

—Galatians 5:6 MSG

If Waterfront Park in downtown Portland was crazy and dangerous, the Capitol Hill area in Seattle was completely occupied territory. In fact, a group of anti-government, "defund the police" protestors who had set up barricades around about six blocks of the neighborhood had recently changed what they were calling the area from CHAZ—the "Capitol Hill Autonomous Zone"—to CHOP—the "Capitol Hill Occupied Protest." Seattle police actually withdrew from the area after clashes with protestors and all but stopped answering 911 calls about fires or burglaries there,[1] as well as shootings and numerous reports of sexual assault before police were finally able to open the area again and clear it out.[2]

It definitely felt like another flashpoint of the craziness America was feeling at the time between COVID and racial unrest after the death of George Floyd. Historic division was ravaging the nation, and CHOP was a prime example of the lawlessness it seemed many of these protestors wanted.

So, naturally, it was the next place we felt God was telling us to go.

Seattle has always been close to my heart; it is the scene of some of my fondest memories from growing up. My family lived in Montana when I was very young, and Seattle was the closest big city; we often traveled there on vacations. I even watched my first NBA basketball game in Key Arena (long live the Supersonics!). I also have many pastor friends in the city who, in 2020, were telling us what was actually taking place on the ground, while news outlets often portrayed it as peaceful protests and potlucks instead of lawless rioters endangering property and businesses in the area. They were downplaying the seriousness of a group cordoning off a section of a city and dedicating it to mayhem, as well as the damage that was being done in the name of "justice" and "equality."

If there were ever a place to worship and pray in America, it was in the epicenter of the violence and anarchy inside CHOP. All of America was watching what was happening in that place. I felt like our mandate was to change the atmosphere through prayer and worship and also to make a statement to the thugs intimidating the masses and wreaking havoc on our nation: "America is *still* a free country! We will not be intimidated and kept from worshipping and praying right in the middle of your 'occupied protest' zone!"

A lot of the people in Seattle had seen what happened in Portland through the viral videos that were being posted, and there was a lot of chatter on social media when we announced we were going to hold an event in CHOP. I didn't know if we would get the same momentum in Seattle as we had in Portland, but it felt like it was only building. Plus, we wouldn't have to worry about permits or police interference because authorities had abandoned the area. It was every person for themselves in CHOP. We knew we were on our own, so we added a few more security personnel, prayed over the event, and headed for the venue.

The level of resistance we faced when we rolled into Cal Anderson Park that afternoon was unlike anything I had ever faced in America. We and three thousand of our friends entered the epicenter of chaos and lawlessness. We were coming to declare that Jesus was Lord over their "occupied territory." Despite the rioters, anarchists, and angry protestors marching, destroying, and bringing violence to the streets every night—enough to chase the police from the area—city officials somehow viewed a peaceful gathering of Christians as a threat. The degree of spiritual warfare going on felt obvious to every person there.

And it was anything but a simple gathering for us. As soon as we got set up, Antifa protestors came out of the woodwork to try to stop us. At first, they shouted at us because we were white, but when three black pastors opened in prayer, they seemed to get even angrier about that. Then they started shouting at us because we weren't wearing masks. They started getting some of their guys to blend in with the crowd, work their way to the front, and then they would all rush in together and try to tackle the drum set and kick over our amps. One guy sprayed Super Glue all over our keyboard and guitar pedals while others tried to drown out our music with bullhorns.[3] At one point, they unplugged a couple of our generators, and all our speakers went silent. But that just made everybody worship harder. The crowd exploded with praise! It confounded the Antifa leaders. The resistance we experienced just caused the fire inside each of the believers gathered to burn hotter and brighter!

Eventually, things reached a tipping point. People gathering to praise God created a human—and spiritual—barricade around the band, and we raised our voices all the higher.

It didn't take long for the very same protestors who had chased the police out of the area to get frustrated because they could neither deter nor silence us. At one point, a guy running one of the livestream channels for Antifa climbed to the top of a hill behind our band and started a crazy rant watched by tens of thousands on his feed. "I don't understand these people," he said as he videoed himself with our crowds behind him. "The more I yell at them, the more f%#*ing fun they have. The more f%#*ing fun they have, man! What's wrong with these people?"

Worship gave way to prayer, and then to preaching the Gospel with joy and boldness. As people responded, we asked if they wanted to be baptized in water troughs we had brought with us just for that purpose, and dozens did. We turned America's lawless hotspot of violence, defiance, and fearmongering into a revival meeting rife with healing, hope, and restoration!

I think it just blew people's minds that so many would show up in a dangerous place like that to worship. It felt like it was a real sign to America and to that region that declared, "The church is bold. We're gonna worship, and we're gonna go after God, no matter what you do!"

As the evening wore on, more powerful ministry followed. We ended up praying for many of those who had come only to oppose

SAN FRANCISCO—This is where it all began. The picture was taken right before our seminal Let Us Worship gathering on the iconic Golden Gate Bridge on July 9, 2020.

The first LET US WORSHIP sign appears at the Golden Gate Bridge.

PASADENA—On the day Los Angeles County officials threaten to fine and imprison people defying Gov. Gavin Newsom's tyrannical stay-at-home orders, four thousand people gather to lift the light of Jesus into the night sky.

NEW YORK CITY—People spontaneously ask to be baptized in the Washington Square Park fountain. Baptisms continue for hours in the most closed city in the nation.

MINNEAPOLIS—Just weeks after the death of George Floyd, God turns a riot into a revival. Salvations, baptisms, and healings break out at the site of his death, displacing the trauma and pain.

REDDING, CALIF.— More than three thousand rally under the Sundial Bridge for one of the most controversial Let Us Worship events of 2020. CNN, Good Morning America, the *LA Times,* and other media outlets vehemently attack those who gather, labeling them "superspreaders."

SAN DIEGO—In scenes reminiscent of the Jesus People Movement of the late 1960s, hundreds of the five thousand people gathered at Cardiff State Beach are baptized in the ocean.

PORTLAND, ORE.— Nearly seven thousand gather in a display of unity and hope at Waterfront Park, just blocks from the area that saw 100 days of nonstop rioting and destruction in the summer of 2020.

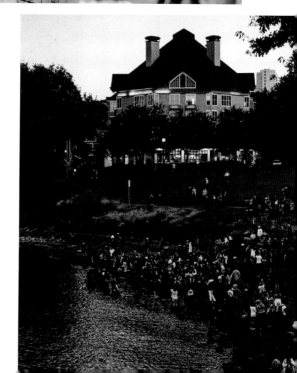

Hundreds of people attending the rally in Portland are baptized under the stars in the freezing waters of the Willamette River.

SEATTLE—A former Muslim (left) runs to the altar to get radically saved in our first visit to the Capitol Hill Autonomous Zone, then dances for the rest of the night in newfound freedom and joy.

SACRAMENTO— More than ten thousand worshippers brave the 110-degree heat and intense smoke from nearby wildfires to lift up the name of Jesus during the height of the pandemic in September 2020.

NASHVILLE—Despite thr venue changes within forty-eight hours and a steady stream of rain, ten thousan people praise God on the courthouse steps. Afterwar the mayor launches a contact-tracing campaign t see how many people may have contracted COVID from the "super-spreader" event; the city is later force to announce that zero case resulted.

SEATTLE—On our second trip to Seattle, after the city barricades Gas Works Park to keep us out, we set up at an abandoned construction site across the street and thousands gather to worship. Federal agents also show up to protect our meeting from nearby satanists, who were found in hazmat suits carrying bowls of blood to dump on the worshippers.

CHICAGO—More than a dozen squad cars and sixty uniformed police barricade the south entrance to Washington Park as we try to set up for Let Us Worship on September 16, 2020.

Despite the worst crime in America, the mayor's draconian lockdowns, and threats of arrest from the massive police presence sent to confiscate our sound gear, we stand firm for God to move. Many are saved and healed, and pastors solidify their bonds of brotherhood.

In one of the most radical moments in Let Us Worship history, a pickup truck with a baptismal tank in the bed spontaneously arrives at the end of our thousand-person Jesus March through the streets of Chicago, and person after person asks to be baptized.

Rolling Stone ran a story online on October 12, 2020. What many saw as more negativity from hostile media was a blessing. "You can't buy that kind of coverage!" a friend told us.

Ro**ll**ingStone

Jesus Christ, Superspreader?

Preacher-musician Sean Feucht stages Nashville concert, ignoring Covid-19 precautions

NEW ORLEANS—The Church is unified as thousands of worshippers from every denomination, ethnicity, and background pack into the iconic Jackson Square near the French Quarter in November 2020. The police voluntarily shut down the street to help us.

WASHINGTON, D.C.—Four thousand people pray on the steps of the Lincoln Memorial before the main Let Us Worship event on the National Mall on October 25, 2020.

The rain, wind, and 40-degree temperature cannot extinguish the fiery love of more than forty thousand burning hearts lifting up Jesus in front of the Capitol. This was the largest church gathering in the world in 2020 . . .

. . . and it came with the strongest response to an altar call at any Let Us Worship event that year. More than a thousand people surrendered their lives to Christ that night.

My daughter Keturah, ten, prays powerfully over the younger generation on the National Mall in October 2020. There is so much hope for Generation Z!

WASHINGTON, D.C.—This new era of revival looks like family. Children will be helping lead the way!

us. It was as if layer after layer of resistance was peeled away. We were able to reach out to protestors in ways the force of the police and the appeasement of the politicians could not.

Most of these people weren't hardcore criminals but had just gotten swept up in the angst of these events, thinking that acting out like this was going to fill a hole in their souls. When it didn't, we were able to reach out with something that did, and many of them responded. (The event was broadcast all over YouTube and Facebook. You can go there to search for videos to see for yourself what that event was like.)

After Portland and then seeing what happened in Seattle, we began to notice a trend: protestors showed up with anger and frustration, but the moment they were met with love and courage, their hardness began to melt away. Some of them were just lost and caught up in a cause they knew little about. Many felt the social pressure to conform and "be angry" or march about something—anything—so they showed up, smashed things, and lit fires. When they came face-to-face with the love of God in our crowds, we helped light a fire in their hearts instead.

It was like we were building an altar in these places so that the faithfulness of God could be recognized as it hadn't been before. We had a growing feeling we were supposed to focus on cities that were in strife and calamity, where nobody had any hope. The more we answered that call, the more it felt like we were empowered to do even greater things.

The days that followed our gathering were a stark contrast to the days before in so many ways. Where the authorities had backed down and caved in to the demands from the protestors, the Church did not. By just showing up and "holding church," Seattle believers took a big step toward taking back their city for Jesus. The scenes and clips from that moment went viral across America over the next several days. It seemed like the sleeping giant that was the Church in Seattle had awakened as three thousand bold worshippers stood up, unwilling to back down from intimidation, opposition, and threats of violence.

No situation is too difficult for God. The more we worship and pray, the more the atmosphere changes in our cities. I think the local churches present at these events saw a new revelation of the true power of the Gospel. When we actually showed up and didn't let anarchists control our streets, we became a force of change and hope that no one else could be. This is not simply us showing up, though—it is the power of the Holy Spirit partnering with our boldness to do the supernatural work that only He can do.

It was so encouraging to see leaders and pastors step up and say, "Hey, we can be the difference here. At the end of the day, if we don't do anything, nothing changes. But if we show up with the power of worship and prayer, if we preach the Gospel, if we love boldly like Jesus told us we should, *everything changes.* Hope breaks in. It's not about politics or ideologies, it's about Jesus. We are at our best when we show up and just let Jesus's love shine through."

Love Changes Everything

"Love" is probably one of the most confusing words in the English language today. It's a word we hear every day in music, on TV, in movies, in ideologies, all over social media, and just about everywhere you turn in myriad ways. It is used to describe the feeling we have when we are drawn to another person, or the bond that holds families together. It sometimes describes how we feel about our favorite stuff, and sometimes it's used interchangeably with "lust." Many proclaim it as the solution to all our problems, because "all you need is love." (It's kind of interesting that the admonition to "love one another" has now changed and lost much of its appeal; many today prefer to shout, "Stop hate!" instead, as if that's really a better answer.)

In this mishmash of misuses, the meaning of love has not only become confused, but even replaced by its opposite. Loving someone has changed from wanting the best for them to accepting them just the way they are, "warts and all." It has become a demand for tolerance and the freedom to do whatever a person wants, even if it is harmful to them. It leads from honoring the "keep out" sign on a teenager's door to honoring barricades put up by protestors that read "no police allowed." Instead of being something that brings people together, it becomes a tool to distance ourselves from one another and even manipulate each other to meet our own selfish desires.

That's just not how I see Jesus's love in the Bible. He gives it a completely different meaning.

The first big difference I see is that, for Jesus, love is an action, not a feeling. We often see Jesus moved by compassion to do something in the Scriptures, but the something He does always reflects the action part of love: teaching, healing, forgiving, correcting, delivering, and even chastising, as He constantly did with the religious leaders. Love was always something He did in reflection of His Father's loving action:

For God so loved the world that he gave his one and only
Son, that whoever believes in him shall not perish but
have eternal life. For God did not send his Son into the
world to condemn the world, but to save the world
through him. (John 3:16–17)

Early in His ministry on the earth, He proclaimed the reason
He was sent:

The Spirit of the Lord is on me,
because he has anointed me
to proclaim good news to the poor.
He has sent me to proclaim freedom for the prisoners
and recovery of sight for the blind,
to set the oppressed free,
to proclaim the year of the Lord's favor. (Luke 4:18–19)

Jesus loved in order to change things. He was never a legalist,
but He never violated one law. He honored faith regardless of
ethnicity, gender, nationality, or title. He went to the sinners—tax
collectors, prostitutes, and any others lumped under a title that
allowed others to pre-judge them—not to accept their wrongdo-
ings, but to transform them and bring them back to God. He
didn't condone the actions of the woman caught in adultery—He
told her to go and "sin no more" (John 8:11)—but delivered her
from the hypocrisy of her accusers. He met a broken, isolated
woman at a well in Samaria who'd been ostracized for her ethnicity by one faction and for her choices by another—"The fact is,
you have had five husbands, and the man you now have is not your

husband" (John 4:18)—and yet He offered her no condemnation, but instead "living water" (John 4:10). And it was in love that He overturned tables and used cords to drive the money changers out of the temple courts, rebuking them: "It is written... 'My house will be called a house of prayer,' but you are making it 'a den of robbers'" (Matthew 21:13).

So, first of all, love is an action. It is something you can see. It is not a feeling, nor is it passive. It isn't an excuse. It always does something, and that something usually looks like stepping into hopeless situations to bring Heaven's solutions. It gives something, it releases something, it sets free, and it sets straight. It nurtures responsibility, not irresponsibility. It restores. It heals. It sacrifices something to pay the debts of others. And it doesn't let evil have its way, but overpowers it with good. It shines a light in darkness. It shows forth forgiveness, that there might be repentance.

If there was anything obvious in the CHOP zone, it was a sense that those who were putting up barriers and acting out wanted something, but it wasn't truly the thing they thought they wanted. They didn't know what to build, so they just tore things down. So much of what we ran into with the protestors and violence in Portland and Seattle (and other places in our travels over the years) was more angst than loyalty to a cause. Taking part in the protests was more about having a place to belong than a true call for cultural change, reversing injustices, or creating space for racial reconciliation. The protestors used their battle cry of "Stop hate" like a bludgeon to punish, instead of using it to clear a pathway to reform.

What was needed was God's love to step *into* the fight and bring healing. Unfortunately, the police didn't have that, nor could the politicians provide it. Instead, it took the Church to step in and be the Church. We needed to show up so that Jesus could shine forth. How do we let Jesus shine forth? We love like He did. We engage like He did. We establish the Kingdom of Heaven on Earth like He did.

Sometimes that seems big and brash, like holding a massive worship gathering in the middle of an area the enemy wants to declare is "occupied territory," whether that is in Seattle, Iraq, or North Korea. ISIS declared their end-time caliphate headquarters were in the ancient Iraqi city of Nineveh (modern-day Mosul). But they must have forgotten the story of Jonah and the testimony of an entire wicked city turning back to God.

The Muslim Kurdish Peshmerga helped us remind them, though, as they invited my team of worshippers to sing and pray together on the battlelines before they took back territory from ISIS in 2015. In North Korea, we were told not to worship, pray, or distribute Bibles, lest we be thrown into prison. Of course, we did all those things, and we did them with great joy as God provided protection to each one of our team members.

More commonly, it's in everyday actions like being in the medical field, rescuing people from human trafficking, working in pregnancy clinics to let people know they have options besides abortion, going into dark places and asking God how to be light, and then simply doing what He's asked us to do. It takes on many different forms in the way we live, the way we act, and the way we do business, govern, and help each other. With our missions organization, Light A Candle, we have rescued almost a thousand children across rural India from temple prostitution, child trafficking, and abandonment. These children were once society's throwaways, yet they are now fully sponsored with housing, food, education, safety, and most importantly, they have discovered that they are children of God and fully loved with a unique purpose and calling.

Love means we act. We do not just watch our cities burn.

If you read my book *Brazen*, you may remember the mansion we bought in Harrisburg, Pennsylvania, to worship in because it was in such a crime-ridden neighborhood. Harrisburg was among the top ten cities in America with the highest crime rates at the time. (The month we were cleaning it up to move in, there was a murder on each corner of the property. Not the best inauguration for a new ministry center!)

A Mennonite church owned it, but the neighborhood around this building got so bad, the Mennonites stopped using it, so we bought it from them. It had been built in the 1800s by a man who planned to have a huge family but ended up childless. It had approximately sixteen bedrooms and five or six bathrooms. It was in pretty bad shape, and even just getting to the front door was gnarly. There was a lot of clean up and refurbishing to do before we could even move any furniture in.

The house number was 333, so we started calling it "The 3–3–3 House."

Once we got things in shape enough to start using it, we began looking around the neighborhood for ways to bring hope, love, and healing to the region. So we started to distribute groceries, and then we started a childcare center for working parents, especially single moms. We organized a men's Bible study and had guys show up who wouldn't darken the doorstep of a church. We brought a group of photographers in and had them go house to house to offer professional family pictures for the community (most homes had never had family pictures taken). We brought in missions teams just to help remove the trash from the alleyways and to plant bushes and flowers. We'd offer yard work to people to help beautify their homes and common spaces. One of the first weekends after moving in, we rallied volunteers for a neighborhood-wide cleaning project. We removed about fifty thousand pounds of trash from the streets and alleyways! The goal was to make the neighborhood beautiful, inhabitable, and full of life again.

The house became such a refuge that people in the community started to protect us. Gangs said it was off-limits for graffiti and other crimes. One afternoon, someone stole a laptop from the house that contained much of the information we needed to keep our projects going. Word got around to the neighborhood about it, and the laptop was returned just a few hours later.

It's amazing what can happen when you take the active love of God into a place and just start doing whatever you can do. It doesn't mean it will be easy or that you won't make mistakes. It doesn't mean you won't get called all kinds of crazy things, from "racist" to someone with a "white savior complex" (sometimes even by the same people). And, of course, results will vary. But as Jesus said, *"My command is this: Love each other as I have loved you"* (John 15:12). It is our job as Christians to love, because, just like the song says, "They will know we are Christians by our love."

God calls us to love like Jesus loved every day, and sometimes God calls us to bold acts of love. It's not love according to the definition of the world, but the love according to our Father in Heaven. Sometimes, it looks crazy. Sometimes it seems wild. Sometimes it plows through barricades—whether they are built in the streets or in human hearts—so that Jesus can get in.

It's what makes us who we are.

SEVEN

BOLD JUSTICE

He has told you, O man, what is good;
and what does the Lord require of you
but to do justice, and to love kindness,
and to walk humbly with your God?

—Micah 6:8 ESV

Minneapolis is a city that is dear to our hearts. Not only is my wife from Minnesota, but the churches from around the region were among the first to invite me in when we launched into full-time ministry after college. We have lots of family and friends there, as well as ministries we've connected with over the years that we work with on a regular basis. It's a city we visit several times every year.

So when George Floyd died while in police custody on the corner of 45th and Chicago on May 25, 2020, it rocked us, as well as the nation. Already months into the pandemic lockdown, the event ignited a racial divide in this nation like nothing seen since dogs and firehoses were used on crowds during the Civil Rights Movement.

I had been invited to speak at North Central University in Minneapolis just a few weeks after Floyd's funeral was held in June.

Our vision was to hold a worship event and pray for unity in the city and the nation. It would be a chance for people to gather, put their focus on Jesus, and call out to God for hope and healing in the middle of a dark time.

I really felt like God was going to use this event to do some good things, but almost immediately there was pushback on social media. Accusations were flying from people saying we were just trying to distract others from the trauma, and that the community didn't need some "white savior" to come in and hold a "concert." While that wasn't our heart at all for Minneapolis, the negative narrative reached a boiling point, and the president of the university finally called us to say they were canceling the event because they were afraid of the credible threat of damage that might arise from protestors gathering outside. But he offered some suggestions on where we might hold it instead and what we should do.

It seemed odd that the idea of gathering pastors and faith leaders of different ethnicities, backgrounds, and denominations to worship God and pray for the city would raise such controversy, but it did. We thought the environment might still just be too raw, and we could easily move the event to another time. So we decided to call off going to Minneapolis for the time being.

Then I got a call from Dr. Charles Karuku, a black pastor in downtown Minneapolis. "You'll never believe what's happening!" he told me. "God is turning riots into a revival!" It turned out the revival meetings he was holding were on the very corner of 38th and Chicago where Floyd had died.

"We are seeing God move every single night with healings, salvations, and baptisms," he said.

Once he had my attention, he told me a bit of the backstory. After Floyd's death, Dr. Charles (as he is affectionately called) began to watch his city unravel into unprecedented rioting, looting, violence, and anger. Angry mobs even burned down the Minneapolis Third Precinct Police headquarters. Charles, whose wife is white and whose children are mixed race, felt the Lord was calling him to go to the site to be a bridge. Heeding this call, he went into the middle of the craziest rioting with prayer and healing to see what would happen next. There was a black church on one corner of the intersection, and its members joined his outreach. When people wanted to be baptized, the church rolled out all its water baptism troughs to the street.

This had been going on for a couple weeks by then, and the group was seeing a genuine outpouring of God's power. Dr. Charles then told me the pastors had all agreed to invite me to come and worship with them. "I feel like you're supposed to be here," he said. "I think it's going to be significant. We would love for you to come."

I said Kate and I would pray about it. As I did, I told the Lord that I didn't want to be a distraction to anything He was already doing down there. That would be the last thing we wanted. "But if You're calling me into this and inviting us into something that You want to do, I don't want to miss Your voice because I'm listening to random trolls online," I prayed. "I want to be obedient."

At first Kate was adamantly against it, but not from fear. She isn't really the fearful type. We had prayed together about me going to North Korea, and she had said I should go. We had prayed together about going to Afghanistan after 9/11, and she had supported it. Even when I applied for a visa to go into Saudi Arabia, she was all for me going if the embassy granted one.

This was different. This felt like we were jumping into the depths of America's rawest racial wound, and who knew what might happen? The backlash just from saying we were going to a college campus in Minnesota had already been like nothing we had experienced before. Did we really want to go through all of that again?

At the same time, though, she trusted me, and she trusted the Lord. So she said if I felt God wanted me to go, she would support it.

I told her I did. I wanted to be part of it, even if all I did there was just witness what Dr. Charles was doing to bring healing and restore hope. So we decided, in the end, I would go and play with their local worship band. No one else from our team needed to join me on the trip.

Because of the backlash we had just experienced, we decided not to announce anything on social media as we normally would; rather, I would just show up and join what the local pastors were doing. So we sort of snuck in—and had a powerful night of worship.

Most of the people present, of course, including the worship band, were black. I just backed them up and led a song and prayers when they asked me to. In the crowd though, I watched as people hugged each other, held hands, and prayed for each other, many of them of different races. So many people were being delivered of pain, sadness, and division in their hearts. It was a beautiful scene.

God was truly making the "Valley of Achor [weeping] a door of hope" as He promises in Hosea 2:15. The spirit of unity among the churches was so strong, it broke the back of the division night after night as people streamed to that street corner from all across the world.

For the first time, I got to see with my own eyes what the nightly news wasn't reporting. The whole area had been barricaded and the police were staying out. The news was reporting on the rioting and violence within the barricades but said nothing about this revival led by a local pastor that was happening on the very same streets. Things were changing on the ground even as the media refused to report this good news! People would come filled with anger, but their anger would melt away as the love of God was released.

These gatherings had so much support from the local community that even rival gangs were declaring the area to be a protected place. There were signs up that said, "No police allowed," but they let the pastors and their worship teams in.

It was powerful to see this happening in the midst of a trauma that was rocking all of America. Here, right in the epicenter of the pain, where the hurting was the worst, God was moving.

Of course, this kicked off even more controversy for us. The rhetoric was the same. People said I was "grandstanding as a white savior," sticking my nose where it didn't belong, using the tragedy of George Floyd's death to build my own brand. All the crazy stuff being said clouded my simple desire to obey God and go wherever He sent me. It was different than when I had run for office, and a foretaste of what was to come. The pushback, the threats, the name-calling, and the hit pieces in the news were only just beginning.

At the same time, I think participating with Dr. Charles Karuku and other Minnesota pastors in that event planted the seeds of what became Let Us Worship and Hold the Line. It helped us recognize the power of taking God's light into dark places in our own nation in the same way we had done for over twenty years overseas. It gave me profound new insight on what it means to call for justice and how the protestors were getting it wrong by trying to achieve those ends through rioting, trashing property, and setting things on fire.

Again, God had a different, truer, and much better way.

"Let Justice Roll Down"

Racial division has been a thorn in America's side since long before the ink on the Declaration of Independence was dry. When the United States Congress could not squelch the injustice of slavery as the nation was founded, the problem lingered until it erupted into a bloody civil war. Men like Frederick Douglass and women like Sojourner Truth pointed to the hypocrisy of a Christian nation allowing slavery and tolerating racism. When Martin Luther King, Jr. delivered his "I Have a Dream" speech, celebrating the hundredth anniversary of Abraham Lincoln's signing of the Emancipation Proclamation, he too called on God for justice, quoting from the book of Amos: "We will not be satisfied until justice rolls down like waters, and righteousness like a mighty stream." (See Amos 5:24.)

It's sad that the call for justice has become such a divisive battle cry today, but that is perhaps because it's a word that has lost much of its original meaning. The term has been weaponized, politicized, and preached from the pulpits across America, but we have neglected or forgotten the root meaning of social justice and need to re-dig the wells of the biblical mandate for justice.

Before I say any more, let's deal with the elephant in the room. Yes, I'm a long-haired Caucasian guy from California who ran for office as a conservative Republican. I believe in the Bible above all, and the importance of family, community, and country. I don't believe you can fault America for the values we were built on—which include "liberty and justice for all"—but there's a great deal that can be said about our falling short of those values.

Some would say I can't speak on this topic because I don't know what it's like to be a minority in America. True, I haven't lived as a black person in the inner city or experienced differing levels of prejudice, racism, and persecution in the same way others have. I am white and have never lived as a black or Hispanic person in America—that's why at every event Let Us Worship hosts, we invite pastors from as many diverse ethnicities who are willing to join us to speak on our stages—including black leaders as well as Asian and Hispanic. It's why we strive to stand together as Christians first, Americans second, and diverse individuals third, doing our best to honor what we all have to bring to the Lord in our various ways. Our events—and the people on our stages—are always multiracial, multi-ethnic, and include as much outreach to the hopeless as we can organize with those who live in those communities.

This, of course, doesn't mean we always get it right. But I have also given more than twenty years of my life to travel to war-torn nations around the earth and help people of all backgrounds, ethnicities, and skin colors. We've rushed into Afghanistan and Iraq to bring tangible acts of love to the refugees feeling terror and suffering because of war. We have rescued almost a thousand children who were homeless, sex slaves, and temple prostitutes across India. Bringing justice to the oppressed is the call of God on every follower of Jesus on the earth. It may look different according to the culture, people, and nation we are focused on—yet the mandate remains the same.

Appearing to be the most compassionate, virtuous "fighter" against injustice on social media is not what drives us; it is *Christ* who compels us. At my core, I am a worship leader and a child of God doing my best to boldly obey Him. Something powerful takes place when we lose our drive to be a "social justice warrior" according to the craving of culture, and we put our hopes on God to right the wrongs instead. We all lift up our voices in praise and our prayers for God's Kingdom to invade the earth. I know no better and righteous justice than the Lord's.

Besides, if you know me, I'm not very good at being silent or avoiding touchy subjects. We can totally disagree on things, and I'm still going to love you because that's what God has told me to do.

So, beyond that, let me say that I believe God has ingrained the cry and the call for *justice* into the very heart of this generation. It is something very special. Everyone is born with a longing to live for a cause bigger than themselves. This is a beautiful, God-given gift to each individual and each generation. Yet without the biblical guardrail of truth in place to bring definition to what *justice* really means, the secular world can hijack the compassion of believers and non-believers alike to usher in social change that ultimately reflects nothing God wants for us.

When this happens, people can start living, marching, and mobilizing for a justice that does not look like Jesus. In the end, it leaves them bitter and angry, and some even abandon their faith because of it. I have witnessed close friends succumb to this over the last few years.

Many called for justice as a form of retribution or vengeance after George Floyd died. That was a tragedy. His killer now has to pay for his deed. That is justice.

But others with darker motives seem to want more. They want to destroy and divide. Some want to malign all police or denigrate an entire race based on the wrong actions of a few individuals. As we saw amongst the rioters and Antifa as we set up for our gatherings, most were just looking for something to be part of, but others were angry and destructive. What should have been peaceful protests calling for justice were corrupted by another agenda and opposition to any kind of rule of law.

It takes boldness to stand up to a mob's thirst for violence. It takes boldness to stand up to the world's readiness to hashtag tragedies for political gain. It takes boldness to advocate for justice in love and not give in to hate, bloodlust, or cheap political attacks.

The answer to healing the effects of such fracturing events is not civil unrest, violent protests, burning down police precincts, or defunding the police, but taking an honest look at what has been going wrong for too long and making it right. It is also resisting the narratives that simply are neither true nor grounded in facts.

Many point to our capitalist society as the problem, but we forget that before Adam Smith—who is often referred to as the "father of capitalism"—wrote *The Wealth of Nations*, he wrote *The Theory of Moral Sentiment*. One does not work without the other. The further we separate morality—*love*, really—from the way we do business or the way we deal with each other, the less any system is going to work. Democracy and capitalism are the best "systems" to use, but that doesn't prevent them being corrupted by moral failure, classism, or any other form of selfishness brought to the table.

"Wokeness" and "cancel culture" are getting it wrong. In fact, this is one of the reasons that many teachers, scholars, and prophets believe the term "social justice" as it is being used today is really just a Trojan horse for a new version of Marxism. To quote economist and social theorist Thomas Sowell, "If you give the government enough power to create 'social justice,' you have given it enough power to create despotism. Millions of people around the world have paid with their lives for overlooking that simple fact."[3] Believers cannot abdicate the call for justice, hand it over to secularized governments to mandate, and then claim this looks exactly like God's justice. That may be the easy way out, but it's not biblical, and it will not sustain lasting change.

We have certainly seen people tried in the court of public opinion and forced to leave jobs, lose public respect, and even be completely silenced with little regard for actual fairness and justice. Whether it's pressure for Spotify to cancel Joe Rogan, the most popular podcast host in American history, for holding a discussion with expert doctors on the corruption behind the COVID vaccine, or the baker in Colorado who refused to make a cake for a same-sex wedding because of his religious convictions, the worldly powers demanding "justice" are mob-like and aggressive. Cancel culture is not only tearing public discourse apart in ways we have never seen before, but also fueling the worst sorts of violence in our city streets across the country today.

We cannot look to government or social media to always reflect what is right and true. We can only look to God for that. You can't legislate change in people's hearts; only God has the power to do that. Certainly, government has its part, but so do businesses, the Church, and nonprofit organizations and ministries. Government programs are never as effective as local communities in helping our neighbors.

No reconciliation, racial or otherwise, is accomplished by shouting profanity across barriers at those with opposing views. What we need is a new understanding of unity, and unity only comes through a very old understanding that real justice isn't possible without the love of God. Even for Christians, following the letter of the law is not as effective as following the Spirit of the law, just as Jesus said in the Sermon on the Mount: "You have heard it said...but *I* say..."

There's no question we have a tough road ahead as a nation, but there's no fixing things without God. It's not going to come from changing our system of government or the values that have made America the greatest nation on earth to live in, warts and all. We do have a lot to fix, but it's only going to come when we all start making more godly choices. We have to resist ditching the values so clearly outlined in our mission statements to opt for the quick buck or abuse our authority to make someone else look smaller.

It's going to take *all* of us to do it. It is going to take our trust in the Lord to bring His justice to our families, communities, and nations.

> The works of His hands are truth and justice;
> All His precepts are trustworthy. (Psalm 111:7 NASB)

EIGHT

BOLD OBEDIENCE

Knowing the correct password—saying "Master, Master," for instance—isn't going to get you anywhere with me. What is required is serious obedience—doing what my Father wills.

—Matthew 7:21 MSG

After Seattle, we received strong calls from pastors and leaders to go to New York. At that point, everything we had done had been on the West Coast, but now we were starting to get calls to hold events in the East. If we were looking for where things seemed to be the darkest and most desperate, New York City seemed a logical next event.

As the fall of 2020 rolled around, New York seemed to be getting hit hardest by COVID. It had the highest number of cases and was the most locked-down city in the nation. As a result, isolation was at its highest, and people on the ground there told us the sense of oppression and fear was palpable.

Not only that, but NYC has also had a special place in my heart, similar to Seattle. My family had moved to the East Coast when I was young, and all through my teenage years, New York was a special place to go. My first missions trip with my youth group was actually to the area—I spent a summer in the Bronx working with a local church. It was also the last place I had preached in 2019 before we knew about such things as pandemics and how one might affect us.

With this first gathering on the East Coast, we felt it would be as symbolic as when we'd had praise and worship on the Golden Gate Bridge—and because of that, we needed a venue just as iconic. Washington Square came to mind, and it made perfect sense.

If you've ever watched a movie set in New York City, especially a romantic comedy, there's often a scene where the couple strolls near the arch in Washington Square or sits on the sides of the fountain there. It is one of my favorite places in the City That Never Sleeps. My wife and I spent many date nights cruising through that park when we lived on the East Coast. In late 2020, it also became a central gathering place for protestors. A friend of mine was doing outreach to them, so it was already being prayed over.

Again, we couldn't get a permit through official channels, but since that didn't stop the protestors, we decided not to let it affect us, either. All the same, we went in with minimal gear. We found a company in New Jersey willing to help us out, and they set up our mics and speakers under the archway.

When the police saw us setting up, they came over to talk with us. When we explained to them we were holding a peaceful prayer and worship event calling for hope and unity, they were incredibly kind and more supportive than any police we had interacted with anywhere else up to that point. A couple of them even said, "We need this right now in the city."

Once again, we had no idea how many people might show up. It seemed to me that the level of fear and paranoia we felt from people there was crazy. All of downtown was locked down and most of the shops were closed as a result. When we started to play, however, people started to join us. It was a smaller gathering than the ones in Portland and Seattle—somewhere between a thousand and two thousand people—but their enthusiasm was just as bright.

The sound echoing off the buildings was so beautiful. Not only was it the most diverse group of people we had gathered so far, it was also the most diverse group of worship leaders and musicians we'd had. We had worship leaders who sang in Spanish. We had leaders who played a more African groove. It was eclectic and joyful, reflecting the best characteristics of New York City itself. You could feel the depression lifting from people as they sang to the Lord.

When I started to give the altar call and asked people who felt hopeless and depressed to raise their hands, almost every single person in the audience did. People started to run forward under the archway where we were set up, kneeling in prayer to give God their depression, their fear, their anxiety, and their hopelessness. For years, we have declared God would give us "The garment of praise for the spirit of heaviness" (Isaiah 61:3 KJV). Here we saw it happening right before our eyes.

During soundcheck that night, a young Guatemalan man was strolling through the park when he heard music. Bewildered, because he had not heard music in the park since the start of the pandemic, he wandered over to take a closer look. He ended up staying for the entire event because he was captivated by the joy and hope of everyone around him. We found out later he had been battling intense depression and suicidal thoughts over the last week. That day in the park, when we gave the altar call, he ran down to the front of the stage and gave His life to Jesus. He came in hopeless and confused, contemplating taking his own life, but found hope, clarity, purpose, and God's heart for him.

After we prayed for him, he immediately asked me, "Now it is time to get baptized, right?!"

I asked him what he meant.

He responded, "Well, I repented of my sin and gave my life to Jesus. Now I think the next thing is to get baptized so everyone can see what happened in me!"

I was floored. Here was a brand-new Christian reminding me of the very thing we had done in other cities, but which I had completely forgotten in New York. He was right, but we were totally unprepared. How were we going to baptize people in a park in the middle of the city? And even worse, how was I going to meet this man's enthusiasm with a lame, "Sorry, we forgot to bring anything to do that with."

Someone behind me who must have overheard his question said, "What about the fountain?"

I followed where he was pointing with my eyes, and there were the famous Washington Square fountains just a few yards way. It turned out they had been closed for several weeks for repair, but just that morning the water had been turned back on and the pool around them was full again.

We notified the NYPD officers standing close by that many people wanted to get baptized and make a public declaration of their faith. We asked if we could use the fountain pool since there was still a high fence around it. "Well, if it's only a couple people at a time, that should be okay," one of the officers told us.

What followed was one of the most beautiful, powerful, and moving baptism services I have ever been part of. One after another, people waded into the water as local pastors prayed with and baptized them. The crowd cheered each time someone came up out of the water, and the worship never stopped.

In a city plagued with fear, death, and disease, this moment celebrating the new life of Jesus inside these new believers stood out. It was the reward for obeying Jesus's "Go," when others thought we were crazy.

The Cost of Discipleship

While it makes sense to many to stay away from "hot spots" of disease, sickness, and depression, aren't these the exact places into which we are called to bring the Gospel, hope, and the Kingdom? Are we not called as believers to drop into places of hopelessness? Does that mean we may expose ourselves to violence, disease, or even misunderstandings of others while we follow Jesus? The answers are yes, yes, and yes.

It reminds me of the mindset required of missionaries early in the twentieth century who packed all their belongings into coffins before heading overseas. It reinforced how real the risks were, whether it be from violence or cholera, dysentery, or some other disease. Many didn't last a month and ended up buried in those very same coffins. And yet they went anyway. They obeyed the call. They stormed the beaches of darkness with the same resolve as soldiers storming the beaches of Normandy on D-Day, but with different aims. Facing opposition and risk in any form shouldn't faze us as much as it seems to do.

Jesus went so far as to say:

> Whoever wants to be my disciple must deny themselves and take up their cross and follow me. For whoever wants to save their life will lose it, but whoever loses their life for me and for the gospel will save it. What good is it for someone to gain the whole world, yet forfeit their soul? Or what can anyone give in exchange for their soul? If anyone is ashamed of me and my words in this adulterous and sinful generation, the Son of Man will be ashamed of them when he comes in his Father's glory with the holy angels. (Mark 8:34–38)

Of course, the real issue isn't the danger or risk; that's not what Jesus is talking about in this passage. That's completely secondary. The real question is about obedience. Each of us has a calling—a cross—to take up. Each of us has our own form of boldness to express. It takes gritty obedience and determination to follow Jesus and take Him at His word. It takes courage and guts. It also takes personal honesty—being able to hear the Holy Spirit's call, acknowledge Him, and then count the cost of action.

The night Jesus was betrayed into the hands of the Romans and Jewish religious leaders, He told His disciples what they were going to face in the hours and years ahead:

A time is coming and in fact has come when you will be scattered, each to your own home. You will leave me all alone. Yet I am not alone, for my Father is with me.

I have told you these things, so that in me you may have peace. In this world you will have trouble. But take heart! I have overcome the world. (John 16:32–33)

In the years following the resurrection, the disciples experienced just that. They panicked in the hours after Jesus said this, but after they were filled with the Holy Spirit, they went into the world and preached the Gospel to all creation. It is the story of the book of Acts. They faced many hardships, including death—history tells us that all the disciples except John were martyred—but they had peace in the midst of it because of their bold obedience to Jesus's call.

And what they did changed the world forever.

But they too had some decisions to make early in their journeys. They faced restrictions of their own. As we saw earlier, governmental authorities told them in Acts 4:18 "not to speak or teach at all in the name of Jesus."

When they did anyway, they were hauled into court again, jailed, and rebuked. "We gave you strict orders not to teach in this name.... Yet you have filled Jerusalem with your teaching and are determined to make us guilty of this man's blood" (Acts 5:28).

To which Peter responded, "We must obey God rather than human beings!" (Acts 5:29).

The Jewish leaders (and it's important to note that Peter and the rest still considered themselves Jewish at this point, preaching about the Jewish Messiah—it would be many years before *Christian* was even a term) were telling them to stop, the government was telling them to stop, they were being thrown in prison, and yet Peter and the believers kept saying, "No. We can't stop. We have to do this. We have to be obedient to what we know is true—to what we have seen with our own eyes and heard with our own ears."

Yes, the Scriptures do tell us to submit to earthly authorities and the governments set over us. As Paul told the Romans:

> Let everyone be subject to the governing authorities, for there is no authority except that which God has established. The authorities that exist have been established by God. Consequently, whoever rebels against the authority is rebelling against what God has instituted, and those who do so will bring judgment on themselves. For rulers hold no terror for those who do right, but for those who do wrong. Do you want to be free from fear of the one in authority? Then do what is right and you will be commended. (Romans 13:1–3)

But here in Acts 5—and throughout the rest of the book—the apostles, and even Paul himself, took a different approach when it came to silencing the Gospel, being banned from meeting with other believers, or carrying out the practices of their faith. Instead, they followed the example of Jesus, who healed on the Sabbath right in front of the very religious leaders who preached against doing any work—even healing—on that day. Jesus even confronted them about it:

You hypocrites! Doesn't each of you on the Sabbath untie your ox or donkey from the stall and lead it out to give it water? Then should not this woman, a daughter of Abraham, whom Satan has kept bound for eighteen long years, be set free on the Sabbath day from what bound her? (Luke 13:15–16)

It's a tough line to walk, but that's what we've been called to discern. We must determine the correct actions to take between obedience to the authorities around us and obedience to God. But this is where I believe these words of Jesus recorded in the Gospel of Luke are the most helpful.

People told us, "I can't believe you're going into New York City. It's ground zero for COVID, so you are putting everyone who comes in danger. You're defying the local restrictions. How dare you! It's so insensitive!" and on and on. But we felt God was calling us to go to a place that was hurting. People in darkness needed light. What would have happened to that Guatemalan man had we not showed up in the park that day? What would have happened to those who were set free of depression, fear, anxiety, and hopelessness? From drugs, smoking, alcohol, or other addictions? From sickness, disease, and infirmity? What would have happened to those who were saved and baptized because we obeyed God rather than the authorities? Would they have found salvation if we hadn't?

These were the fruits of our obedience. What would have been the fruits of our disobedience? It's impossible to say, but I prefer knowing the former to settling for the latter. If we go and free the bound despite what authorities say, even do it right in front of them, isn't that the example Jesus gave us in this passage? We must each follow our own consciences in this, but if we are to walk in love, if we are to be restorers of hope, if we are to shine forth God's light to those who need it the most, we decide according to faith, not fear. We must go above and beyond to do good. We must act according to what Paul wrote in Romans 13:10, just a few verses after telling us to be obedient to the established powers: "Love does no harm to a neighbor. Therefore love is the fulfillment of the law."

Right after Kate and I got engaged, she left to attend a YWAM missions school in Hawaii while I was finishing college at Oral Roberts University in Tulsa, Oklahoma. When we spoke, we'd talk about what we wanted to do for our wedding. Our parents had agreed to help in small ways, but for the most part, it was up to us. We wanted to have something big enough to invite close friends and relatives, but we weren't sure what it would look like beyond that due to a lack of funds.

Back in high school, Kate had gotten into a really bad car accident. A guy ran through a red light and hit her nearly head on. Her entire head went through the windshield, and she ended up with 120-some stitches in her forehead. She had pieces of glass embedded deep in her scalp that had to be removed, and she underwent laser surgery on her head and face. She also received a settlement from the courts. It wasn't as much money as it might have been today, but it was something. She had planned in her heart to spend that money on the wedding and reception that we wanted.

A while later, the mission school held a send-off ceremony for all of those going out to the nations in the next season. Families came, and all the current students and staff were there; it was a big celebration. Near the end, administrators asked those who were still in need of finances to come in and say how much they needed to raise so they could obey God in their call to the missions field.

"We want to pray," the leader of the school said, "and ask God to bring breakthrough so that all of these will be able to go on their outreaches."

Kate felt a tug on her heart. In response, she emptied her entire savings account, including her settlement money, and gave it so that all those families and students could go on their missions trips.

I was furious when she told me.

"These people can't stay here," she told me. "They've got to go to the nations! They've got to go reach the lost! I couldn't *not* help! Why am I even in school if I don't support people to go?"

I told her I thought they'd made an emotional plea and taken advantage of her. Now how were we going to pay for our wedding?

"Sean," she said evenly. "The Lord spoke to me, and He said, 'I am your Father. Fathers take care of weddings, and I am going to take care of this.'"

I had no response.

And it turned out, she was right. Long story short, there was a series of other miraculous circumstances that provided more than enough money for the wedding and reception that we wanted. About three months before the wedding, Kate had gotten a job at a very upscale restaurant on the beach in Virginia Beach—a miracle in itself to get, since she was only twenty and knew nothing of alcohol and wine, which were the big sellers—and she made good money and got great tips, which gave her a small nest egg for miscellaneous expenses. We were given the use of a church building that held up to eight hundred people—free of charge!—and a couple volunteered their time to cater the desserts for our reception.

(We didn't do a full meal.) Then my dad donated some frequent flier miles towards our honeymoon, which was enough to get us to Venice, Italy. And that was just the beginning of the many ways God has provided for our family as needs have arisen over the last two decades. We've seen His faithfulness over and over again—the fruits of our obedience when He's asked us to do crazy things.

We want no sins of omission. We want no help from Heaven denied because we hesitated to obey the Lord. Fear has no place in godly decision making. We don't run away from darkness; we run directly into it! We don't hide from sickness; we believe in the One who alone can bring healing. We don't shrink back when things get difficult; we rise up! This is what God was teaching us all through the journey of Let Us Worship, and what I believe He is continuing to teach us even as I type these words at the beginning of 2022.

And I don't believe it's going to change in the years to come. It's only going to get harder. We're going to have to get better at discerning the voice of God from the white-noise confusion of what the world around us is saying. We're going to have to get bolder in obeying God.

Because what's to become of the people of this earth if we don't?

NINE

BOLD GRATITUDE

*Rejoice always, pray continually, give thanks
in all circumstances; for this is God's will for you
in Christ Jesus.*

—1 Thessalonians 5:16–18

From the day we planned to meet on the Golden Gate Bridge to pray, we felt we needed to declare, "This state belongs to Jesus. The Church is alive in California. May God's presence fill this place! May a new Jesus People Movement start here and spread to the rest of the nation." With that still in mind, after our Los Angeles event, we started seriously exploring the possibility of holding a Let Us Worship gathering on the steps outside the California State Capitol building.

I reached out to a friend in the state legislature to see if she could help us obtain a permit for the event, and she agreed to sponsor us. It was September 2020, wildfires ripping across the state were filling the air with smoke, and temperatures were soaring over 110 degrees. So when she asked me how many would probably attend, I tried to overestimate the numbers. In the past, we had helped mobilize similar prayer and worship events in Sacramento.

I led worship at one of them, The Call Sacramento, in 2010. It often took many months (and sometimes years) of hard work to rally even four thousand people to show up for these gatherings, especially in Northern California. This was also on short notice (about three weeks), the weather was awful, and the skies were choked with smoke from the wildfires raging nearby. So I said, "Maybe like five hundred to a thousand?" thinking that would be the most we might get if we worked really hard at spreading the word.

At the time, Sacramento was the most locked down of the locked-down places—especially the Capitol grounds, from whence all the California mandates were originating. Sacramento is known as a very politically left city that has produced key legislation for the Golden State that includes no-fault divorce, abortion, and same-sex marriage. It leads California—and because of California's forty million residents, fifty-three congressional districts, and fifty-five electoral college votes, whatever comes out of Sacramento is likely going to spread across the nation.

Despite the simplicity of what we were trying to do—come together outdoors, worship God, and pray—it turned out to be significantly more difficult to rally the churches around this event than I thought it would be. When we reached out to churches in the area to invite their congregations, many refused; some even told us we were being irresponsible to invite people to gather in clear disobedience of governmental mandates. Others didn't even respond. It felt like a lot of Christian leaders didn't want anything to do with us.

From what we had experienced elsewhere, though, we knew people needed an opportunity to gather in God's presence. We felt the deep conviction that if we showed up, God would show up as well and meet the people hungry enough to come out. In many ways, if felt like a big expense to have a full sound system, screens, and our entire setup for several hundred people, but we knew deep within ourselves that it was the right thing to do in a very difficult time for so many. This was the most expensive Let Us Worship gathering we had ever pulled off at that point. It also was the first event we set up with high-end HD cameras for a legitimate livestream.

Our permit set our start time at 4:00 p.m., the hottest part of the day; by 2:00, it was already 111 degrees. (Our band's computers on stage were fried and would not restart due to the intense heat.) The smoke from the wildfires was so thick, you could hardly see five feet in front of you. When you drove down the street, you had to have your hazard lights on so people could see you.

By 3:00 p.m., though, six thousand people were already waiting for us to get started. By 4, there were more than ten thousand. It was completely overwhelming. It far exceeded the limits of both our permit and the police presence we had on hand. It also exceeded the number of volunteers we'd recruited. We had no idea people would show up to sweat like they did. In addition, hundreds of thousands of people watched online.

About halfway through our time, prominent Sacramento-area pastor Sammy Rodriguez took the stage to preach, and prayed words that really summed up the heart of the event:

> Right now, if you turn on, if you connect to ABC, NBC, CBS, MSNBC, CNN, Fox, Univision, or Telemundo, right now you're going to hear the sound of a nation in a state that is broken. A nation in a state filled with fear

and angst and consternation. Separated, divided by dis-
cord, political, cultural, racial, [and] economic melees—
it's just a collective sort of hysteria.

And the Lord said, "Tell them about the sound."
Because out of Sacramento, California tonight, there is
a different sound... The next sound that will fill the
earth will not be a pandemic, it won't even be a political,
cultural movement. The next sound to fill the earth will
be the glory of Jesus that will fill the nations...

I hear the sound of Ezekiel 37:7—the rattling of bones
coming together... I hear the sounds of the bones of the
Church coming together. I hear the sound of black, white,
yellow, and brown coming together!

And I want to remind you, on these steps, I'll push
back on every spirit that tries to divide us. There is no
such thing as a white Church, a brown Church, a black
Church—there is only one Church: the Church of Jesus
Christ!...

I hear the sound of pastors and worshippers, prayer
warriors coming together, I hear the sound of a Church
that understands there is no such thing as...comfort-
able Christianity. There is no such thing as complacent
Christianity. There is no such thing as politically correct Christianity.

I hear the sound of one Church telling the Pharaohs
of our current age, "Let my people go so they may worship!" I hear the sound of one Church bringing down the
Goliath of hatred with the stone of love...

I hear the sound of a Church standing up. I hear the sound of a Church ready and poised to change the world. A Church that will lead the way. So therefore, I hear the sound of one nation, under God, indivisible, with liberty and justice for all![1]

Pastor Charles Karuku from Minneapolis was there with us as well, and told the crowds:

This is the time to come together. We cannot allow the enemy to divide us, we cannot allow him to use division by politics. We cannot allow him to divide us along ethnic and racial boundaries. The white, the black, the brown must come together. We cannot allow him to divide us along the lines of those who wear the masks and those who don't wear the masks. We are one Church, we are one people, and only a united Church can heal a divided nation. This is the time—let the healing begin!

Honestly, we left Sacramento realizing the Church has left her buildings. God moved with such power that night. We had so many salvations, there were people lined up for baptism around the Capitol Building. People were healed. Addictions were broken. It was an amazing time.

And God wasn't done yet. What happened that day in the California State Capitol opened door after door, until we finally found ourselves standing on the National Mall in Washington, D.C., just weeks later.

And none of it would have even happened had not it been for an act of bold generosity just a month or so before, back in Los Angeles.

Money, Money, Money

It is often difficult to see what God is doing in the moment, and perspective is often not obtained until somewhere down the road. That is the case as I write today, a year and a half after these events, reviewing the journey of Let Us Worship. It would be easy to look at the events we held for Let Us Worship in the summer of 2020 and see them as a well-organized, politically motivated response to the shutdown mandates that were happening across our nation, as well as around the world. Some have suggested we were just taking advantage of the situation to build our following and get into the public eye to garner more donations.

While it is true that our organization survives mostly on donations and these events can be quite expensive to stage, that never really entered our minds—especially in those early weeks. First of all, until we started planning for Sacramento, we never really thought far beyond the next event. Sometimes we would just announce the next event (like D.C.) before we even had a venue, permit, or resources to pull it off! I was actually considering closing the whole thing down because of all the fuss we were causing, and until we went to Los Angeles, we never asked for offerings at any of our events. In fact, it wasn't even my idea to ask for one in L.A.

As I mentioned a couple of chapters ago, our drive down to L.A. from Redding for this event was a difficult one. Kate really wanted us to stop holding these events and quite honestly, to stop wrecking the nice lives we had established for ourselves as worship leaders and missionaries. My congressional race had beaten us up, and we needed some time to heal. Though I fundamentally disagreed, hearing my wife share her pain and knowing that what I thought I was hearing from God might mean going against her concerns was one of the hardest moments in my life. I had to take them both into consideration. I had to be absolutely convinced God was calling us to do this, or I needed to give it up.

Each of the events before Los Angeles was pretty much organized in a few simple steps:

1. Call a few friends in the area.
2. Announce we were going to be in a certain place at a certain time.
3. Show up with our little portable loudspeaker and just start singing with whoever was there.

Then maybe someone would call us from another area and ask us to do the same thing there, we'd load up the handful of equipment we had, and we'd do it all over again. If we had more than we brought, it was because a church, local musician, or band in the area provided the sound system, etc. (as the Slavic church had done in Portland).

Any expenses accrued beyond that, we just covered out of pocket—mainly because I was just burnt out on fundraising after the congressional run. That had felt like one big fundraising journey up until the day I lost. I raised more than $350,000 for everything from TV ads to flyers, and it seemed so pointless. I worked harder than I ever had before to raise money just to throw it into the machine that is American politics today. I pretty much asked everyone I had ever met for money. Good friends were not even taking my calls anymore because they knew what I was calling about. (And honestly, I can't blame them!) So I was certainly ready for a break from having anything to do with fundraising, and I was taking one.

That was the situation when we rolled into that cul-de-sac in Pasadena on July 23, 2020. Once again, I fronted the money for the event, even though I knew that wasn't sustainable. It felt like one more reason it might be time to call it quits.

But near the end of that Pasadena gathering, that all changed. A buddy of mine from L.A. jumped on the stage and told me, "I feel like we're supposed to do an offering."

My mind raced. We didn't have any buckets or ways to collect checks and cash. We didn't have a merchandise table where people could give with their credit cards through an online system—which would have been impossible anyway, with so many people. I was at a loss for how we might do that.

Before the event, however, he'd asked me to set up a Venmo account—a money-transferring app we'd never used before. I had done so under the account name "Let Us Worship." At the end of the event, he came onstage again and asked everyone in the audience to get out their phones and told them how to give an offering to Let Us Worship through Venmo. "We're going to bless Sean," he said. "We're going to cover the price of all this gear. And we're going to give enough to cover their next location."

That night, with their heads bowed over their phone screens, people in the cul-de-sac started giving on Venmo. It absolutely floored us. We could not believe it. I didn't even know it was possible to do an offering like that. Because I hadn't thought to turn off the notifications, my phone started blowing up with announcements about each individual donation—until it finally gave out and just died. The flood completely sapped all the power out of it.

When I was finally able to plug my phone in and get enough juice for it to come back on, I saw there was more than $20,000 in the Let Us Worship Venmo account, and I was floored all over again. Can you believe that?

That night we had announced that we felt like we were supposed to take this movement to Sacramento, even though we didn't have plans beyond that at the time. As if the spontaneous offering weren't enough to encourage that, a businessman in the audience came up and told me, "Hey Sean, I heard about this worship thing you were doing here tonight. I had no idea what it was, but I came out here in the street and I experienced revival. I have never seen the power of God move like this before—especially in the streets. My wife and I were truly touched. If you want to go do this in Sacramento, we'd like to give enough to cover whatever it takes."

Suddenly, any excuse I thought I had about quitting because the events weren't sustainable was gone. In the same bold way God had said He was going to cover the cost of our wedding all those years ago, now He was telling me He was going to cover the cost of Let Us Worship.

It was such a bold night of generosity that it forced me to reconsider any ideas we'd had about stopping. In the midst of everyone losing their jobs or going home without pay until businesses owners knew when they could reopen, we received the most spontaneously generous offering I'd ever experienced. It felt just like how the

Macedonians gave to support the church in Jerusalem, which Paul wrote about in 2 Corinthians 8:2–3:

> In the midst of a very severe trial, their overflowing joy
> and their extreme poverty welled up in rich generosity.
> For I testify that they gave as much as they were able,
> and even beyond their ability.

As I mentioned a couple of chapters ago, I believe God has engrained the cry and the call for *justice* into the very heart of this generation. There is an incredible sensitivity to wealth gaps right now—how unfair it is that the rich get richer while the poor get poorer—and it feels like some people naturally assume that if you've made a good deal of money, you must've done something wrong, like you've somehow manipulated people to part them from money that would be better spent feeding their children or paying their rent. (Even if, as in our case, we use the money that comes into our Light A Candle organization to feed lots of children and rescue them from a devastating future.)

It's the narrative we read in the scold war on social media, but it's also an issue that is as old as the Bible itself. Jesus spoke more about money than anything but salvation. Whether you have it or not, it tends to be a thorn in people's side if they don't think about it correctly. It somewhat goes without saying that people accept that "money is the root of all evil," even though the Bible doesn't say that (unless, of course, you cut "the love of" from the verse—"the love of money is the root of all evil"). The narrative that someone is only doing something because of the money they can make from it is so prolific it's often accepted without thought—even though most of the people who believe it then turn around to go to a job they wouldn't do unless someone was paying them to do it.

As a worship leader and former (almost) politician, I have seen both sides of what money can do. Raising money for a political campaign was strange; it all seemed to get wrapped up in feeding a divisive fight. Millions are raised and spent on those campaigns, and except for providing some jobs, the money actually seemed to do very little for the people those politicians were supposed to be helping. As a missionary, when an outreach or missions trip was sponsored, I got to see the tangible results of that generosity almost immediately, and for a long time afterward, in the lives touched and changed, in children fed and housed, and in churches established in new places.

In each case, though, to think of money as anything more than a tool to get something done is to deify it into some kind of magical, often corrupting force—as if having money pass through your hands, regardless of what you are doing with it, somehow dirties you, and that you must have done something manipulative to get it. I believe this kind of thinking fuels much of the lean toward socialism we see coming out of our universities today; younger people tend to believe that the only answer for the wealth gap is some kind of government redistribution of wealth. (That is another oversimplified narrative that gets many of the complex issues about what creates poverty all wrong.)

Don't misunderstand me: While I think the U.S. has the best system of government and ways to grow an economy in the world today, I don't believe it is perfect. I would never have agreed to run for political office if I thought things were fine the way they are.

Much needs to be fixed, but I have seen more good accomplished by touching hearts with the Gospel than in anything political I have ever done.

Whether in business or ministry, I have learned that to keep money from getting the best of you, you have to first approach it as a tool to do what you are called to do. Then you have to choose an attitude of gratitude for what you have been entrusted with, rather than see it as confirmation of your greatness, which will only make you feel entitled to spend it on your greed.

One of the downsides of capitalism as we practice it in the U.S. today is that we are constantly told through advertising that our best self is on the other side of our next purchase. Want a bright smile? You need this toothpaste. Want a great lifestyle? You need this car. Want to be healthier and look fit? You need this exercise machine, these special supplements, and only buy the most expensive products. As a culture, we are constantly being told we are not enough, and the reason for this is that we simply don't have the right stuff.

The only way to really flip that script is with gratitude for what we have and where we are now, and knowing the only real treasure worth having is the one Jesus spoke about:

> Do not store up for yourselves treasures on earth, where moths and vermin destroy, and where thieves break in and steal. But store up for yourselves treasures in heaven, where moths and vermin do not destroy, and where thieves do not break in and steal. For where your treasure is, there your heart will be also. (Matthew 6:19–21)

As country singer Willie Nelson has repeatedly said, "When I started counting my blessings, my whole life turned around."[2] According to psychologist Robert Emmons, a professor at the University of California-Davis who is leading a long-term research project on the effects of gratitude, being more grateful can change our lives. Research has even shown that gratitude increases self-esteem, improves relationships, and reduces stress.[3] I know from personal experience that it can have a lasting positive impact if we practice it every day.

We are currently living in what is possibly the most entitled and ungrateful time period in history. Lack of gratitude has almost become a virtue worth celebrating in our day! Never has a generation had more wealth, freedom, and information at their fingertips than right now. World Wars I and II and the Great Depression have long been forgotten. The conveniences and comforts afforded by the sacrifice of prior generations have created people who do not recognize how they got to where they are.

Entitlement has become a cancer in our culture. Millennials and Gen Zers often feel we have the right to be offended and "triggered" by anything we dislike, whereas older generations seemed to have more grit and resolve to press through discomfort and tension. I can speak about this because I am a millennial and employ almost all millennials and Gen Zers across my three nonprofit organizations. While we have *more* of everything than almost any generation in history (resources, access to information, etc.), the focus always seems to be on what we do not have. Yet this is not the calling or mandate of the Kingdom of God. Thanksgiving and gratitude are always the doorway for increase. This is true in our lives, families, businesses, and ministries.

Nothing I have experienced in my life compares to the thrill of boldly obeying God and then seeing Him confirm our obedience by showing up and changing lives. It is true that where He guides, He provides. I have seen it too many times not to know He is always faithful. If I looked at His provision with an attitude of entitlement, there is no doubt it would go to my head, so I choose instead to be grateful with what we have and always view it as enough to do what God is calling us to do.

TEN

BOLD IDENTITY

Who is going to harm you if you are eager to do good?
But even if you should suffer for what is right,
you are blessed. "Do not fear their threats; do not
be frightened."

—1 Peter 3:13–14

L os Angeles was one of the cities that invited us to return. The people were in desperate need of hope. The lockdowns had crushed their spirits, shut down the churches, and isolated everyone. The riots and unrest had fueled violence across the greater Los Angeles area unseen since the '90s. No one knew more about this devastation than my friend Matthew Barnett of the Los Angeles Dream Center, a large outreach organization downtown that caters to the homeless, addicts, and needy. It is widely known and respected across the city for its work. It had been hit hard by COVID, losing many volunteers due to the restrictions as its cash flow dropped significantly while needs multiplied. People had no work, kids were home from school, crime was exploding in the streets, and the ministry was stretched super thin on all margins. There were lots of needs, and not many resources to meet them.

When pastors in the region called to invite us, I told them a big part of my heart was to come alongside the Dream Center and help raise money for it. We had some other friends running a ministry not far from Skid Row, called Azusa Street Mission, that we wanted to help as well. We had been working with them for years. So we started to dream about what it might look like to do various outreaches around New Year's Eve to help them. The homeless population was in dire need because almost all the organizations that had previously been helping them were shut down. Homelessness was a crisis exploding across California and tent camps were located across L.A., but many people were afraid or unable to help them because of the pandemic.

We decided to join forces and do an event near the exact location where the Azusa Street Revival began back in 1906, a second outreach on Skid Row, and a third event in Echo Park near the Dream Center. The grand finale would be a Let Us Worship event for believers around the world to gather for worship, prayer, and celebration as the clock struck midnight on New Year's Eve. There was no better way to ring in 2021 than worshipping with thousands in L.A.

When we announced our plans and the outreaches leading up to it, people on social media went crazy. Protestors came out of the woodwork to try to shut us down, force the city to intervene, and slander our names online. The message was basically, "I can't believe you white colonizers are going to come to Los Angeles with your plague and infect the homeless."

Despite the opposition, we started raising money and made preparations to bring food and clothing to be distributed to those in need. We wanted to go into the heart of this dark and desperate situation to bring worship and hope. The community itself was open to this, but the noise from the fringe elements was loud.

The night of the event, people seemed to come from all over to stop our outreach. There were thirty or forty cars parked near the intersection of Fifth and Towne trying to block us from getting into the Skid Row area with our equipment and the resources we were bringing. People were screaming that we didn't have masks on, even though most of our crew did. We even had a team lead worship with masks on, but that seemed to make little difference to the protestors. (It didn't really seem to matter that so many of us weren't white, either; they still kept up their "white colonizers" rhetoric.)

Protestors shouted all kinds of insults at us as we set up, began to play, and handed out food and clothing. They called us "super-spreaders" and said we were just there to exploit the homeless. They pepper-sprayed some of our worship leaders in the middle of a set. They honked their horns and shouted obscenities, trying to drown out the singing.

The next morning, we transitioned east to Echo Park, just a few blocks from the Dream Center. During the worship set, protestors who had been recruited from outside the area to disturb, disrupt, intimidate, and commit violence charged the band when we started, trashed the drum kit, and toppled the speaker stands—but the people kept worshipping the entire time. A homeless guy who lived in the park, who had responded to an altar call earlier in the day, actually tackled one of the protestors trying to wreck our equipment, shouting at him, "We want and need these guys here in our city!"

It was evident to everyone present that the people we were helping wanted us there; the only people who didn't were those who had a divisive agenda. We were just doing what God had called us to do: preaching the Gospel and trying to bring help and hope where it was needed most.

In moments like that, you really have to know who you are. We were facing all kinds of opposition—not only on social media, but in the streets and from government officials who actually fined us for this series of events. (Think of it: we were fined by the city of L.A. for handing out food to the homeless!) People were disparaging our names, intentions, organizations, and whatever they could think of to shout profanity about. We were navigating a field of virtual land mines on the front lines of America's culture war, and we had to watch every step we took.

Our final stop was the Let Us Worship New Year's Eve celebration in Valencia, a suburb about thirty-five minutes north of L.A. Three news helicopters circled us the entire four hours of the event, broadcasting to the world that the "Christians" were gathering for a superspreader event that was going to endanger the lives of many and even kill innocent people.

In the end, we were able to raise $90,000 and donate it to the Dream Center to help build and furnish a brand-new wing for a rehabilitation center for single mothers. We passed out hundreds of pounds of food on the streets. It was a powerful and impactful time together because Los Angeles was one of the most locked-down cities in America. Here we saw more clearly than ever the demonic agenda to steal, kill, and destroy people during the pandemic. Never before had we seen such opposition to us helping the people we were ministering to. We'd had people shout at us and try to stop our worship and prayer, but this was the first time people tried to block us from feeding the hungry or clothing the needy.

Such experiences really shake you and make you question who you are and what you are doing. Had we not known that we belonged to God, that He was calling us to do this, and that the opposition we were facing wasn't really about us as much as some larger societal angst motivated by darkness and emptiness, we might have wavered. The streets of Los Angeles are no place for people unwilling to be bold. It really gave deeper meaning to the words of Isaiah 50:7:

Because the Sovereign Lord helps me,
I will not be disgraced.
Therefore have I set my face like flint,
and I know I will not be put to shame.

Because we didn't back down, we fed hundreds and saw multiple salvations, healings, and deliverances from addictions. Hope crashed into the hopeless that day, and we are still hearing the testimonies of all God did. That event ignited something in the city as well: it sparked a church movement of people gathering to worship in Echo Park that is still happening every week to this day.

The Culture War

When it feels like every force in the world rises up with immense opposition to label you, box you in, and define you on their own terms, you discover the power of your identity in Christ. When you set out to do good and every force imaginable steps up to oppose you, it takes a kind of boldness rarely seen to keep you on track. But that is the kind of boldness we must have to stand against the accusations and bring the Kingdom of Heaven to the earth. This demands a boldness of identity the world neither knows nor understands.

Since the first days of Adam and Eve in the Garden of Eden, the battle has not just been about who we are, but *whose* we are. In Genesis 3:4, the serpent first approached Eve with a direct attack on her identity through questioning what God had already said:

> "You will not certainly die," the serpent said to the woman. "For God knows that when you eat from it your eyes will be opened, and you will be like God, knowing good and evil."

The story has not changed between then and now. Our enemy is using the same old tricks to bait a generation into sin and shame through denying the truth of what God has already spoken, that *"God created mankind in His own image"* (Genesis 1:27)—that we are His image bearers, to be like Him in what we create and build.

The enemy wants to attack our confidence in acting upon that image set deep within our hearts. He wants us to question our position and purpose in the sight of the Lord. He knows that if he can destabilize our identity, he can thwart the incredible destiny and calling that is on each one of our lives. He wants us unsure and striving, never certain of the affection, insight, and acceptance from God that we have been freely given already!

1 John 4:29 reminds us that *"We love because He first loved us."* It is not because of our good works, our revelation, or our knowledge that God loves us. We cannot work hard enough to gain

His affection and earn His favor. He loved us in spite of our faults, insecurities, and sin—and before our hearts were even turned towards Him. This is the power of His grace toward us, and it cannot be taken away. It is possible, however, that we doubt it to the point that we never fully step into who He has called us to be.

One of the most remarkable and life-defining moments Peter faced as a disciple was when he responded to the public opinion poll Jesus gave His disciples: *"Who do people say the Son of Man is?"* (Matthew 16:13).

They told Him the rumors circulating around town—or you might say, what was flooding the Twitter-like gossip feeds of the day:

"Some say [you are] John the Baptist; others say Elijah; and still others, Jeremiah or one of the prophets."

"But what about you?" he asked. "Who do you say I am?" (Matthew 16:14–15)

Jesus was not asking them about the most recent polling data or the latest media narrative about Himself. He wanted to know the truth of what they believed! Who did they really believe He was?

At that point, Jesus had spent nearly three years pouring everything He had into these twelve men and those who journeyed with them. They walked, talked, ate, and lived together while the disciples collectively witnessed the greatest miracles performed before their very eyes by God Himself! This question was the ultimate test to see if they finally carried the full revelation of what He was born for, lived for, and eventually died to bring. Herein lies the question we all must answer to truly discover our own identity that will ultimately unlock our destiny.

Peter answered for the group, *"You are the Messiah, the Son of the living God"* (Matthew 16:16).

Ding, ding, ding! The victory bell from Heaven rang as all the exhausted angels working overtime to help Peter breathed a sigh of relief! (I am only kidding, of course, but the reality is that Peter—one of the more impulsive among the group—finally got it right!) After all those walks with Jesus along the dusty roads of Galilee, the nighttime discussions below the stars, the sermons, the miracles, and the truth being spoken over him again and again, Peter was finally and confidently able to profess the truth of who Jesus was.

As soon as this powerful profession was released, Jesus turned the tables on Peter and began to tell him who *he* was. The "ah-ha" moment of Peter's life made way for the greatest revelation of his identity.

> Jesus replied, "Blessed are you, Simon son of Jonah, for this was not revealed to you by flesh and blood, but by my Father in heaven. And I tell you that you are Peter, and on this rock I will build my church, and the gates of Hades will not overcome it. I will give you the keys of the kingdom of heaven; whatever you bind on earth will be bound in heaven, and whatever you loose on earth will be loosed in heaven." (Matthew 16:17–19)

Peter's true identity was unlocked in this moment of confession. He was no longer just a fisherman from the small town of Bethsaida in Galilee; he was a rock with a firm foundation rooted in God. He also carried the keys to open doors and shut doors, to bind and to loose. He was a man with a secure purpose and a powerful authority. Though he would waver more than once in the years to come, Peter always returned to the path God had set for him, and as a result, the Church is what it is today.

We need to do the same in our day. Our purpose is equally locked up in our identity, and that identity is only rock-solid if we know Jesus for who He truly is and walk as His disciples, just as Peter and the other apostles did.

You would have to be living under a rock these days not to see the culture war that is raging for the hearts and minds of the next generation. It is a direct attack on the kind of identity Peter formed in this moment. There is a spirit of confusion, chaos, and anxiety working overtime to pervert, distract, and destroy the identity of our sons and daughters while making them question everything the Bible says about who they are. It is a false message that hasn't changed since Satan tried to convince Eve that she could gain all the knowledge she needed without God's help—that truth and peace are found internally, and not externally through the person of Jesus. That justice is defining what we are against and attacking it, rather than defining what we are for and contending for it.

We should not be surprised that this war is upon us. We should not be alarmed. The prophets warned of it, Jesus confirmed it, and then He commissioned His followers to leap into the heart of it! It has always been around, yet it feels as if it's getting stronger and stronger as we approach the end of the age. For example, my children have to battle things at their tender ages that I never had to face growing up in the 1980s.

The attacks on gender, family, and any and all absolutes established in the Bible have never been more intense. It is a full-on attack on who we are and what it means to be a follower of Jesus. Satan knows that if we never discover who we were created to be, then we can never fully step into the destiny of what we're meant to do on the earth. Like Peter, we need a revelation from Heaven to illuminate our minds and shatter the oppressive blanket of doubt and hopelessness hanging like a cloud over the upcoming generation.

If we, God's people, don't persist in helping, who will? And what will happen to those who need love and hope the most?

Suicide rates were skyrocketing toward the end of 2020, drug and alcohol use were at all-time highs, and often victims of domestic violence were locked inside homes with their abusers. The most difficult and sad reality was that churches were closed as well. During one of the darkest and most depressing seasons in modern history—yet one more time when the Church was meant to bring light, hope, and healing to overcome uncertainty and chaos—too many church doors were closed. As discouraged and frustrated as I was during this season, I knew complaining about it would not get us anywhere. As I learned from the churches of Afghanistan, Saudi Arabia, Iraq, and North Korea, the Gospel cannot be silenced—it must take action.

I knew the resistance we would face when we took our private affection for the Lord into the public square would come in many waves. What I did not expect was how many "non-church" folks would flock to our gatherings. Much of this was due to the decision to host these gatherings in the very hearts of culture and the most locked-down and oppressed cities. Although it would have been easier to stay in the suburbs or rural areas, I knew our call was to bring the Gospel to the darkest, neediest places.

This gave way for what I love to call "collateral damage." This is when people who weren't even planning to come strolled by and were affected by the atmosphere of love, power, and the presence of God rising from our events. Just like when everyone in the prison was freed by the sound of Paul and Silas praising God (see Acts 16:16–40), He often uses the few to affect the many.

I believe God is bringing a fresh wave of revival across America. This is not about working harder to receive God's love and affection, but understanding the power of abiding in His love.

One of Jesus's most profound teachings on identity comes from John 15. Speaking to His disciples about why He came to Earth right before He was about to give His life on the cross, Jesus said:

> I am the vine; you are the branches. If you remain in me and I in you, you will bear much fruit; apart from me you can do nothing. If you do not remain in me, you are like a branch that is thrown away and withers; such branches are picked up, thrown into the fire and burned. If you remain in me and my words remain in you, ask whatever you wish, and it will be done for you. This is to my Father's glory, that you bear much fruit, showing yourselves to be my disciples. (John 15:5–7)

Every single human being longs for significance, for meaning, and to have "fruit that remains" in their life. In these verses, Jesus cracks the code of significance. He gives us the key to live a life of meaning, purpose, and bold identity. It is all about abiding in the vine!

This revelation kills the notion that we need to perform for approval and work harder to produce fruit to please our Father in Heaven—or that somehow, we just don't measure up to what Jesus is calling us to do. But we are not alone. All identity and meaning comes from abiding in the vine.

How do we abide? By spending time with God in praise, worship, and conversation (prayer). This is the opposite of a culture trying its hardest to climb the ladder of significance through self-promotion and performance, as we see so often in the world around us. God's answer to identity is to rest in His presence. As counterintuitive as it may seem, the key to knowing who we are is wrapped up in the words God spoke in Psalm 46:10: "Be still, and know that I am God."

Just as we saw with Peter, the key to knowing who we are lies in knowing who Jesus is. In fact, it was Peter who wrote: "His divine power has given us everything we need for a godly life through our knowledge of him who called us by his own glory and goodness" (2 Peter 1:3). That is all we need to know to step into a bold identity that cannot be shaken.

ELEVEN

BOLD UNITY

How good and pleasant it is
when God's people live together in unity!

—Psalm 133:1

Leading up to our national meeting in D.C., we also had events planned for Nashville and New Orleans. Both turned out to be powerful, monumental times for Let Us Worship. They took place just weeks apart, and they both drew an insane amount of scrutiny and backlash. There was more animosity from city mayors than we had experienced before.

We had yet to do a Let Us Worship event in Tennessee at that point, but several leaders and pastors had asked us to do one in Nashville, which is a city with a lot of churches, worship music, and a strong Christian presence. The minute we announced our date to go, there was immediate pushback, which caught us a bit off guard. Nashville's culture is vastly different from places such as L.A.'s Skid Row or even downtown Portland. There were so many shut-down churches and ministries in the area and we'd had so many invitations, we thought people would be excited that we were coming.

One of the most unexpected opponents was Mayor John Cooper. We had already secured a permit from the city to hold our event in a downtown park, but when Cooper got wind of the event, he spoke against it. The city then canceled our permit just two days before the event, sending us scurrying to find another venue fast.

We found a private indoor venue and began talking with the owners about holding it there. I didn't really want to go indoors because it was hard enough to have an outdoor event—but there was rain in the weather forecast, and it was large enough to hold the number of people we expected. But after the city found out about that, someone called and threatened the owners with massive fines if they agreed to move forward. I received a call the day before our scheduled date from the manager of the venue, apologizing for the fact that they couldn't afford to let us hold the event there.

So I was again faced with a dilemma: We had a call from God to go to Nashville, pray for unity, and preach the Gospel, but we had no venue. We tried to set up in another park, but that got blocked as well. Maybe it was finally time just to let it go and move on to the next city.

The thing was, we hadn't canceled an event yet, and we had been in much darker places than Nashville. How could we back down? There had to be an alternative. Along our journey, I had been hearing a phrase that proved true in this case as well: *The greater the resistance, the greater the breakthrough!* Usually when we are facing this much struggle to pull off an event, it reveals a spiritual struggle that we sometimes cannot see. Those events end up being the best and most fruitful if we simply have the determination and grit to follow through.

As with most major cities, Nashville had had several protests in recent weeks; theirs had been held in a big grassy area downtown in front of the courthouse. When someone suggested we have our own "worship protest" there, it just made sense. So some twelve hours before we were scheduled to start playing, we switched our venue to the courthouse.

Between that, all the negative press about the event, and the rain in the forecast, we had no idea how many people might come. As we were setting up, a friend from the area—a black worship leader—came up to me, bursting with enthusiasm and hope. This was exactly what I needed in that moment of weariness. He had mobilized a big part of the community to attend and was excited that the event was back on.

"We gotta do this, even if it rains, even if they try to shut us down again, let's just do it!" he told me. "We'll just focus on what God is gonna do in the Spirit and not what happens in the natural."

By the time we were set up on the steps of the courthouse and ready to begin, more than ten thousand people had gathered. It blew everyone's minds.

One of the funny things about Nashville is that it's a hub for both Contemporary Christian Music and country music, and we got more support from the country music artists than the Christian ones. They really showed up for us, posted on social media about it, and told all their friends how amazing it was. Several of them were there. They seemed as blown away by the number of people who came as we were. One of them told me, "Man, Garth Brooks could announce that he's doing a free concert in downtown Nashville—at the courthouse—and he wouldn't have gathered ten thousand people! How'd you get so many to come?"

Of course, we all knew it was a miracle. Only God could have pulled off something this powerful and this last-minute in the face of this much resistance.

We had an amazing evening. Several pastors and a lot of worship leaders from the area showed up and prayed and sang with us. (Again, you can see it all on YouTube, including how big the crowd was.) Many people were touched by God's presence. Something about being all together in the midst of the crazy cultural climate was removing fear from all who attended.

During the altar ministry time, a homeless man wandered in from the street and mixed in with the crowd, listening intently. At the altar call, he came down front, lifted up his hands, and started screaming, "I want Jesus! I want this Jesus!"

It ignited a chain reaction.

People everywhere started coming forward to give their lives to Jesus. Drugs were dumped from people's pockets and thrown onto the stage as spiritual chains of addiction were being broken. We prayed against depression and for those battling suicide, addiction, and fear. Then we began baptizing people; the baptisms went for hours, with a line stretching around the entire plaza. It ended up being one of the longest Let Us Worship events we ever did, lasting well over six hours.

Of course, in the wake of the event, the media went crazy with its takes on what we had done. The next day, *Rolling Stone* magazine had me on the front page of its online edition with an article titled, "Jesus Christ, Superspreader."[1] Despite the somewhat negative tone of the article, it included a video that reflected the diversity of those who attended and took the stage, as well as us worshipping, praying, and baptizing people. Initially, I was dismayed about the article and called a friend, a well-known artist who is used to both positive and negative press. After checking out the link I sent him, he laughed hard into the phone. "Bro, you could not even pay for this kind of publicity!" he said. "This is absolutely incredible! What an epic name too! *You are the Jesus Christ Superspreader!* Congratulations!"

Meanwhile, the mayor of Nashville took even deeper offense with us. He sent investigators to talk to the organizers and the guys on the ground who'd helped put things together—including sound people and some of the worship leaders. The city also launched a contact-tracing program to determine how many people may have contracted COVID from attending the event. Administrators were fully locked into the superspreader narrative and poised to announce high case numbers connected with the event. They wanted to further shame the Church for gathering to worship Jesus while they applauded and encouraged the racial protests. The mayor announced a press conference in advance to share how our gathering had spread the virus.

But when he held it, he actually seemed a little disappointed to announce there had been no positive results for those who had attended and been tested. And while the media had been all over us in the days after the event, none of the news outlets published any retractions as far as I know. Still, it was pretty great to hear from someone who had spoken so adamantly against what we were doing and made such a big deal about investigating our "superspreader" event that the investigation, in fact, found no new cases connected to those who had attended.

When that announcement came, though, we were already on to our next planned outreach in New Orleans. The pastors there collectively chose a location downtown to host our gathering in Jefferson Square, not far from Bourbon Street. It is a historic and meaningful location where former presidents had given public addresses.

New Orleans ended up being our most diverse gathering since New York—probably even more so. We had black churches there, Hispanic churches, Cajuns, and more. Christian music artist Lauren Daigle showed up and sang with us and ended up getting barred from being part of the 2021 *Dick Clark New Year's Rocking Eve* broadcast because of it. She later released a statement in response to her removal:

> Out riding my bike with a friend, I saw [New Orleans Police Department] barricades set in place and uniformed police officers providing protection for a gathering of people that had come to pray. I was asked to sing. To me, that is the very moment when music serves its higher purpose. It's what gives people encouragement, hope for a better future, and it's what can usher joy into their hearts. My involvement was focused on lifting spirits, providing hope, and encouragement during these polarizing times.
>
> I'm disappointed that my spontaneous participation has become part of the political discourse, and I'm saddened by the divisive agendas of these times. I would

have been, and still would be, honored to represent our city on New Year's Eve and although I was aware of discussions regarding my involvement, an offer was never made. I have wept, pleading for this chaos to dissipate and for harmony to return. We need unity when people are desperate, suffering, starving, or out of work.[2]

And our event did bring unity. Many of the churches from around town had not done anything together for many years. We had a pastors' luncheon before the gathering, and they agreed to set differences aside and pursue revival for their city in such a difficult time. "We need it," one pastor said. "Now is the time we need to break through all the fear."

So many people showed up at the outreach that the police had to block off the main street through the French Quarter. While we would have expected the police to be upset with us, it was just the opposite: they commended us for holding a peaceful gathering. They even asked us if we wanted them to block off the entire street. I told the officers, "Do whatever you think is best, but we want to serve the city and not disrupt things." He looked at me and said, "This unity, this love, and this music is serving our city! We're gonna block the street off so more people can attend."

They had no problems with us, but Mayor LaToya Cantrell went ballistic. She held press conferences every day for a week or two following the event and absolutely slammed us. She called me out by name, called out my friend and singer Lauren Daigle, and criticized several of the pastors involved, accusing us of hosting a superspreader event that would infect and kill many people. It seemed inconsistent, because she had marched with Black Lives

Matter protestors and held a big victory rally for Joe Biden after the presidential election with a lot of unmasked people present. Yet, the church was a perpetrator. She quoted Romans 13 several times about the church obeying government authorities, as I have—but it was taken out of context and felt manipulative, especially when other gatherings were still happening in public places and she wasn't saying a word said about them.

During the event, though, we saw God show up again in tremendous ways. First of all, it was incredible to see the pastors and churches come together in unity to lift up the name of Jesus. The church of New Orleans had been battling division for many years. Many church splits, relational fallout, racial tensions, and just plain bad rumors had plagued the leaders of the region. Yet this became one of the greatest times of healing it had ever experienced. When the city needed God, they pulled together to help. The pastors continued to remind me weeks after the event how historic and profound it was.

We also saw many miraculous healings take place. A pastor's daughter with a brain tumor who had been having horrible seizures came forward for prayer, and all the area pastors laid hands on her. It was a moment of great humility and breakthrough. We later learned she had stopped having seizures from that day forward. It was miraculous, and the people in the city are still talking about it. Testimonies from New Orleans kept rolling in long after we had left, and the boldness the attendees stepped into changed things moving forward. Churches began to open and held follow-up gatherings. It felt like the name of the Lord had never been shouted louder in Louisiana, and we were glad to have played a part in God touching the state.

Unity in the Spirit

As Christians, I believe we have the best unifying tools on the planet in worship and prayer. When we come together in the name of Jesus to praise our God and pray for each other, our nations, and the world, ideological differences have a way of losing their divisiveness. When we come together at the foot of the cross, we discover that we have far more in common than what sets us apart. The media focuses on conflict because that gets people's attention and buys them clicks online, but we are not called to live according to that divisive spirit.

The default attitude in our culture today seems to be to put *me* over *we*. Social media and network news resonate with people looking at what they *don't* have and blaming those who *do* have those things for their lack. They make much more noise about the color of a person's skin than the content of their character. They obsess over race and identity politics.

But when we come together at the foot of the cross to worship and pray, all of that becomes secondary to the commissions Jesus gave us to make disciples and to establish the goodness and blessing of Heaven on the earth.

By giving our lives to Jesus, we join an incredibly multifaceted family. We trade earthly limitations for spiritual possibilities. We join in a common cause to obey the voice of the Spirit of God in each of our unique ways. As Paul wrote:

For those who are led by the Spirit of God are the children of God. The Spirit you received does not make you slaves, so that you live in fear again; rather, the Spirit you

received brought about your adoption to sonship. And
by him we cry, "Abba, Father." (Romans 8:14–15)

Embracing diversity and tolerance for differences seems to be
one of the loudest cries of this generation. There is a strong call to
right historic wrongs. This is good. But many of those who shout
the loudest on social media and in our universities tend to get this
call backwards. They often focus on the outward attributes of a
person rather than the inner attributes. You don't have to look far
to see this desire—no, this demand—for external diversity in
everything from TV commercials to films to TikTok videos to
political appointments. The trouble is that this type of diversity
focuses almost exclusively on the outside.

Let me be clear: God made every race, ethnic group, and culture on the face of the earth. In doing so, He used a wide, beautiful
canvas of colors, distinctions, and attributes that lift up the unique
beauty of people across the globe. Our external attributes reflect
the creativity and love of a wonderful Creator! However, nowhere
in His Word does it say we are to fixate on the external. We are to
look toward the inner heart and character of a person.

Does this erase the fact that racial and ethnic injustice and
tragedy have plagued humankind since the dawn of time? No! God
grieves over racial hatred. He mourns when one people group
elevates itself over another.

But it is only through biblical unity—unity built upon the words
and life of Jesus—that true reconciliation takes place. The world's
ways are not enough. We have seen over and over again the failure
of humankind's attempts to define and execute justice and equality

devoid of God's heart, Word, and mind. The Crusades. The Holocaust. The Gulag. And on and on down through history.

That is the critical distinction I am trying to make: it is only under the shed blood of Christ that unity—true, lasting, godly unity—can come about. Jesus called us to be peacemakers (Matthew 5:9). Peacemaking is very different from peacekeeping. British Prime Minister Neville Chamberlain attempted to keep the peace with German Chancellor Adolf Hitler, and we saw what happened there. It took a Churchill to stand up to evil and fight it with everything at his disposal. Similarly, in the current spiritual war we are fighting against beliefs and ideologies that starkly oppose the Word of God, we must first fight on our knees, and in praise and worship. These are our greatest tools against Satan's blitzkrieg.

We all play our part in this spiritual war. For example, when things looked dire for Great Britain during World War II, a man named Rees Howells gathered an army of intercessors to stand against the Nazi invasion of the United Kingdom. Many leaders in Britain recognized this prayer army as a critical key to the nation's ability to withstand Hitler's war machine. (I highly recommend the book *Rees Howells, Intercessor* by Norman Grubb, which tells this miraculous story.)

While peacekeeping is temporary, Jesus's brand of peacemaking is eternal. We know that while we fight daily battles, the outcome of the war is certain: Jesus wins! He is the peacemaker.

Today, we see unbiblical practices and models of tolerance that make strong calls for us to conform to certain ideologies and accepted narratives. And here is the lens through which all of us must view another person's form of tolerance: there is always blame and shame for those who think differently. Consider the fruits of the Spirit outlined in Galatians 5. This is the yardstick by which God asks us to approach the very critical issues of diversity, tolerance, and social justice:

> But the fruit of the Spirit is love, joy, peace, forbearance, kindness, goodness, faithfulness, gentleness and self-control. Against such things there is no law. Those who belong to Christ Jesus have crucified the flesh with its passions and desires. Since we live by the Spirit, let us keep in step with the Spirit. Let us not become conceited, provoking and envying each other. (Galatians 5:22–26)

Of course, we must start with ourselves. Are we holding ourselves accountable in our words and actions? Is our own house in order? Are we loving our wives, families, friends, and yes, even our enemies, the way Christ taught us to? It starts with us—the Church, and those whom God has called to a higher standard. (That higher standard is to conform our lives to Christ—not to presume that we are better than others.)

But indeed, you don't have to look far to see the finger-pointing and calls to cancel those who don't toe one of many anti-biblical tribal lines. In such cases there's no forgiveness or tolerance at all. That's not real unity or diversity. It's a counterfeit.

God's Kingdom is different. We are not called to conform to each other's opinions, but to the example of Jesus's obedience to His Father. We are called to join together in following the leadership of God's Spirit. We are called out of slavery to the fears of the

world—out of bondages to addictions, phobias, and "lifestyles"—
and into freedom in Christ. We are told wisdom begins by fearing
only God because that delivers us from every other kind of fear.

When we are led by the Spirit, we find the intimacy of calling
on our "Abba, Father" (rather than "Abba," we would probably
say "Daddy" today), and the diversity of being part of His family
and His Body. This unity is not just external, but from the heart.
It's the only place where all are truly welcome, there is forgiveness,
and our differences sharpen each other's iron (see Proverbs 27:17)
rather than everyone getting bullied into conforming to the same
ways of thinking and the same blame-shifting irresponsibility.

David paints a picture of what God's family should look like
in Psalm 133:

> How good and pleasant it is
> when God's people live together in unity!
> It is like precious oil poured on the head,
> running down on the beard,
> running down on Aaron's beard,
> down on the collar of his robe.
> It is as if the dew of Hermon
> were falling on Mount Zion.
> For there the Lord bestows his blessing,
> even life forevermore.

I think the beauty of true unity in the body of Christ (see 1
Corinthians 12:12–30) is the diversity of the people, the diversity
of background, diversity of ethnicity, and the diversity of callings
and responsibilities. We don't all think alike, and God created us

this way on purpose. In Christ, there is great diversity of thought and background, but unity when we contribute to each other and to the common cause of Kingdom-building using our unique identities—the callings, giftings, experiences, backgrounds, educations, and talents that have been given to us. As Paul wrote elsewhere, focusing on the external is a mistake. It is unity in heart and spirit that matters.

> For there is no difference between Jew and Gentile—the same Lord is Lord of all and richly blesses all who call on him, for, "Everyone who calls on the name of the Lord will be saved." (Romans 10:12–13)

> There is neither Jew nor Gentile, neither slave nor free, nor is there male and female, for you are all one in Christ Jesus. (Galatians 3:28)

> Here there is no Gentile or Jew, circumcised or uncircumcised, barbarian, Scythian, slave or free, but Christ is all, and is in all. (Colossians 3:11)

As we traveled to cities across the U.S., we saw that we were not nearly as divided as people think. That really is a media-driven façade. It's a scheme of the enemy to keep us divided and keep us in our corners so that we don't come together and accomplish the work of building God's Kingdom. We all want success for our families and safety in our cities. We want God to be in our lives and in our communities. We don't want crime. We want to be free to follow our own callings and build wealth and stability as our gifts and talents make possible. We want to be healthy and happy.

Whether you're a Republican or a Democrat, conservative or liberal, white, black, Hispanic, Asian, Samoan, or any other ethnicity, the common denominator for all of us is coming to the foot of the cross together, and then going out and doing what He's called each of us to do. That's how unity works. Paul wrote, "From him the whole body, joined and held together by every supporting ligament, grows and builds itself up in love, as each part does its work" (Ephesians 4:16).

Overcoming our differences by clinging all the tighter to Jesus is where bold unity flies in the face of the narratives that blame and shame others, making us feel powerless instead of coming together and actually fixing things.

We saw this in the crowds that gathered at every Let Us Worship event. They were as diverse as you can get racially, politically, and ideologically, but they all came to lift up Jesus with the same hunger for His presence—and that made all the difference in the world.

We didn't have to spend a lot of time at the beginning of each gathering trying to convince people that we weren't who the media was saying we were. Our identity and motivation were not in being "superspreaders" or "attention-mongers" or far worse things. Instead, we just lifted up the name of the King of Kings and let Him pave the way in people's hearts. Worship and prayer create common ground. It is the oxygen of Heaven for the breathless souls on Earth.

Worship is where we lay down our rights, lay down our lives, lay down our agendas, and lay down our allegiances and ideologies.

David likened unity to precious oil poured out on our heads and flowing down off our chins. Why? Because oil is sticky. It goes everywhere, it's hard to wash away, and it smells good. When we're unified, it's like an oil that flows over us and spreads the fragrance of the love and Spirit that we carry. The whole world can smell the unity.

In the last public prayer Jesus prayed over the disciples and those who would follow Him because of their message, He asked:

> I pray…that all of them may be one, Father, just as you are in me and I am in you. May they also be in us so that the world may believe that you have sent me. (John 17:20–21)

Jesus lays out the true key to His kind of unity—bold unity—which is to be as close to Him as He was to His Father when He walked the earth. That's a pretty high calling. But we see the power of it every time we see the disciples in "one accord" throughout the book of Acts. They were in "one accord" on the day of Pentecost when three thousand people joined the church within twenty-four hours. They continued "daily with one accord in the temple.… Praising God, and having favour with all the people. And the Lord added to the church daily such as should be saved" (Acts 2:46–47 KJV). They prayed with one accord in Acts 4, and the building they were in shook. (See Acts 4:23–31.) In Acts 15, they came together in one accord to make a decision that opened the Gospel to the whole world. You can study it for yourself: Every time they came together in unity, God moved amongst them.

I don't believe that has changed today, because I have seen God show up too many times when we came together to lift up His name in one accord! That's the bold unity the Church will need if we are going to be part of God's revival at the end of the age.

We need to show the world that we stand together despite our backgrounds. It is what this generation really wants, but they are falling for a counterfeit diversity because they don't know the real kind. It's up to us as the Church to show them God's genuine plan. Only a unified church can heal a divided nation.

TWELVE

BOLD WITNESS

On my account you will be brought before governors and kings as witnesses to them and to the Gentiles. But when they arrest you, do not worry about what to say or how to say it. At that time you will be given what to say, for it will not be you speaking, but the Spirit of your Father speaking through you.

—Matthew 10:18–20

As we moved toward our event in Washington, D.C., those who had opposed us upped their condemnation. The first time my family received actual death threats was after New Orleans. It was a little scary, but it also felt like we must've made some kind of breakthrough that was threatening the enemy more than ever.

These came in the form of countless direct messages to me that flooded in over Twitter, Facebook, Instagram, and email. Some were graphic, threatening to kill my children and rape my wife.

Kate received many of these as well, so she got off social media entirely for much of 2020 and 2021. Trolls would send her messages saying things like, "Your family and your husband will die soon!" or "You will get what is coming to you and we will make sure you never see the sun again!" The worst and most invasive were the voicemails, text messages, and personal letters sent to our home with similar threats that were too graphic to write out here. We notified the social media companies and restricted, banned, and blocked thousands of the accounts these messages came from—but they continued to come. Our neighbors knew of the threats that came by mail to our house and were on high alert to watch after my family while I was traveling.

One of the most powerful effects of God showing up when we stood up for Him was that we continued to see unity come. Walls separating people of different ages, races, denominations, and classes came crashing down. The common denominator was the presence of God; we met under that banner, and our hearts fell in sync with His. We saw that develop and grow with each new outreach.

For example, when we were invited to Chicago, we joined with a black church, a Hispanic church, and a Russian church to do an outreach on the South Side. The crime rates during the pandemic were exploding and the tension from the lockdowns was palpable. Yet Mayor Lori Lightfoot was ordering police to block church parking lots with their cars so members could not gather to worship God. It seemed that her desire to stop live worship in churches was a higher priority than the crime overtaking the city streets!

We chose to meet in a park in a very rough neighborhood in South Chicago where we thought we would have no opposition. When we arrived, however, we were met by twenty to thirty police cruisers and a couple of SWAT-type vans. The deputy chief of police, a black woman, was there to speak for city hall.

When we pulled in to set up, she came straight over to talk with us. She told us her squads had been instructed to confiscate any gear from our trailer the minute it touched the ground, and then fine us. If we continued to try to set up, we'd be arrested.

We huddled together to figure out a plan. Dr. Charles Karuku from Minneapolis was with us, and he was almost excited about the possibility of getting arrested. In fact, he said if we decided to proceed, we needed to wait until he ran back to the hotel so he could put on his suit. That way he would look his best in his mug shot!

The police, meanwhile, just stood and waited.

As we prayed about what to do next, I remembered the word of God to Jehoshaphat when Judah faced a mighty army. He said, "For the battle is not yours, but God's" (2 Chronicles 20:15), and "You will not have to fight this battle. Take up your positions; stand firm and see the deliverance the Lord will give you" (2 Chronicles 20:17).

I grabbed my guitar. "You know what?" I said. "Let's just do this acoustic."

More than five hundred people had already gathered, so there was no way everyone would be able to hear us, but we just went with it. We yelled for everyone to come to the front, and I told them, "We're just gonna worship and sing with an acoustic guitar. We don't need a sound system. We're gonna trust the Lord to bring the breakthrough."

So we started to worship, and the crowd began to grow. Again, it was a racially diverse group—and it wasn't just young people, but mothers and fathers from the churches who helped carry the event with us. It was beautiful to see everyone lifting up the Lord together as we sang. It seemed to really touch many of the hearts of the officers standing by as well. It started raining lightly that night, but we just kept on singing.

After a few songs, we began to pray, and it was evident that people in the back couldn't hear. So who retrieved a megaphone from her car and offered it to us to use to broadcast the prayers?

The deputy chief of police.

Of course, this fired the crowd up even more, and everybody cheered for the police. It was a powerful moment and shifted the atmosphere of the entire night.

The deputy chief later confided that she was a believer and was moved because we kept worshiping even though we only had the acoustic guitar. That wouldn't have happened had we been defiant and unloaded our sound gear. I'm so glad we trusted God to fight the battle for us. I really believe that He is always speaking to us, even in the intense moments of life—and if we'll just make space, we can hear Him.

We led the rest of the gathering that night using the deputy chief's megaphone. I actually led worship with someone holding the megaphone to my mouth while I played guitar. It felt like something we would do a on wild mission trip!

At one point, a bunch of white protestors showed up, and they were filled with rage. When one of the black pastors took the stage and started preaching, they got eerily quiet. When he gave an altar call, specifically calling out people who needed deliverance from a spirit of offense, some of them came forward and gave their lives and their offenses to Jesus!

We had made no plans to baptize people in Chicago as we had done in other cities, but a truck with a big tub in the back filled with water pulled up at the very end of the event just so we could baptize people. It literally came at the perfect time. A line formed and we started baptizing people in the back of the pickup truck. A few of the protestors even got baptized! We finished the night with a thousand person-strong Jesus March through the crime-ridden streets of South Chicago.

We experienced a similar spirit of unity when we were in Atlanta in October 2020, gathering under a massive warehouse roof during a lightning storm. Something started in Chicago that we did not want to lose, and it affected every city from that point forward.

When we went back to Seattle that fall for an event in the iconic Gas Works Park, this heart for unity brought breakthrough in some of the most difficult circumstances. The mayor of Seattle used taxpayer money to fence and barricade the entirety of Gas Works Park (which is massive) just so we could not use it to gather to worship God. A group of local pastors had been holding prayer walks around the park to prepare for our event—and when they discovered the fence just before we were scheduled to hold a sound check, everyone rallied together to find alternatives.

During our first Let Us Worship in Seattle, we had just had a couple of pastors with us, but this second time we had close to twenty. Some thought we should tear the fences down and hold the event in the park anyway, but my team and I felt it would be better to find a different venue.

As it turned out, there was a construction zone adjacent the park that appeared to have been abandoned due to COVID. The street was being repaved and construction equipment was everywhere, but it was clear that no work had been done for some time. The entire street was blocked off, creating a place where we could gather thousands of people, so we decided to move there.

It turned out to be a better alternative because people could hear us from the street, shops, and nearby restaurants. Many people in the area wandered over, curious about the music and the crowd. God was able to move on their hearts, and we are still hearing testimonies of what happened there to this day. We made numerous media headlines again because we refused to back down and still gathered, even if it was outside the barricaded park.

That event was also significant because the Seattle police didn't show up, but several federal agents came. When I asked them why, they said, "We're not here to shut you down. We're here to protect you." One of them even pulled up his sleeve to reveal a cross tattoo on his wrist.

It turned out they had heard that a group of Satanists were planning to show up in hazmat suits and throw blood on the band as we played. The Satanists did show up, but thankfully, because the federal agents were there, they were prevented from reaching us with the bowls of blood they were carrying, and nothing interfered with what God wanted to do that night.

One of the most powerful and unifying moments I have ever experienced took place in L.A. around New Year's Eve 2020. As I mentioned earlier, we worshipped and prayed in the exact location where the Azusa Street Revival started in 1906. One of the remarkable things about that revival is that it happened when a black man, William Seymour—a one-eyed, thirty-four-year-old son of former slaves—came together with people of various races to wait on God and to pray. When these believers gathered in one accord, allowing God to erase the color lines with the blood of Jesus, an encounter occurred that would forever rock the world: a rush of the Holy Spirit filled each meeting, reactivating the gifts of the Spirit in the Church in a way that it hadn't experienced in centuries. The events of the Azusa Street Revival launched the Pentecostal Movement and the Charismatic Renewal, saw thousands of churches planted, and innumerable healings in the century since then. It also birthed a Spirit-filled missions movement that would affect almost every nation on earth.

A friend of mine, the late Fred Berry, was a black pastor of a church near the Azusa Street site. When he heard we were coming, he called me and said, "Man, we need to drive a stake in the ground. We need to remind everybody of the revival history of the city of L.A. We need to remind people about Azusa Street. You know, God will not move in our city or our nation outside of a spirit of unity, and that revival is a great example of what can happen when we all come together."

So we agreed to work together, and held meetings to pray together to see what God might have us do. We called leaders together to mobilize their people to stand in the gap on behalf of their cities and to quell the violence of the protests and riots. On the day before our big New Year's events in L.A., we planted a unity tree together on the site of the Azusa Street Revival. We prayed that this would be a prophetic sign to show the fractured City of Angels that we were coming together to build something redemptive for the generations.[1]

It was a powerful ceremony. A reverent hush fell over the crowd when Fred and I took shovels and started digging together. After we planted the tree, I told Fred that my kids would grow up watching it thrive and would bear witness to another historic revival of unity. I felt the weight of it that night as a prophetic act.

He smiled with outrageous Fred Berry joy and said, "Let it be, Jesus! Let it be!"

When we returned hours later to that same location to worship and pray, we honored Fred before the crowd and talked about the planting of the "unity tree" as a memorial to the history of revival in Los Angeles, and the hope of what God was still going to do there. It was especially impactful because Fred passed into glory less than a year later, but that tree will live on—honoring the work he did and the prayers he prayed over that region.

Breaking New Ground

When you're called to pioneer and take new territory for God—whether it be a new place or a new atmosphere, such as we were experiencing in the midst of COVID—there isn't always a roadmap or a blueprint for what to do and how to do it. You have to believe that the Lord is calling you to do it, and when you obey that calling, your boldness sets an example that encourages other people to be bold as well.

Sometimes I look back and think that the most dangerous virus spread during the pandemic wasn't COVID-19, but fear. Yes, COVID was real and a considerable threat, but so were the effects of rising depression, drug use, and suicidal thoughts due to the isolation and lack of work for too many. Just as there was a need for wisdom in the response to COVID, there was a need for a response to fear. In such harrowing circumstances, courage is needed to breach the silence and help those in need, wherever they may be. That kind of bold example becomes contagious in its own right.

What we wanted to spread in each city we visited was the bold Gospel, following the example of the early Church. This was the example I was following when I went into areas that seemed the most closed to the Gospel around the world. I already knew what opposition looked like. My encounters with the church in Afghanistan, the church in Saudi Arabia, the church in North Korea, and the church in Iraq encouraged me, and it was their examples I had in mind as we tried to encourage others across America and the world in this season.

It was rewarding to see groups emerge that wanted to keep the fires of worship and prayer going in the regions where we hosted our gatherings. A group of teenagers in Southern California began to gather regularly after we had a local event. A worship leader who had played with us at an outreach began to take what we were doing and gather smaller groups on beaches, in malls, and even in subways. We saw this ripple effect happen all across America. We also saw movements erupt in places like Canada, Australia, and across Europe—some of the most locked-down places in the world.

As all this was happening, I was also surprised to meet Christians in our travels who had been encouraged by my congressional run and decided to run for office themselves! Over the last two years, I've met about thirty people who ran for city council, mayor, state office, and even for the U.S. Senate. Even though I had failed in my run (or at least I thought I failed), it wasn't about me winning my race. It was about having the courage to do something that seemed beyond hope. Success is not determined by outcomes, but by obedience.

As I mentioned at the beginning of this book, the days following my election defeat were very dark. Now, however, I was beginning to realize that new ground had been broken because I ran. People were encouraged by my effort, even though the result was not what matched my human expectation at the time. Behind the scenes, God was using my congressional run to give others the courage to seek political change themselves.

It's hard to fault what is happening in government if we are unwilling to be involved in it ourselves. I understand that not everyone is called to run for state or national office, but perhaps God is prompting you to join the political campaign of someone whose values match your own. If we grow weary and give up our voice, it allows those politicians taking advantage of the current pandemic to continue in their agenda to silence our voice in the future and to take away our freedoms.

It's humbling to think that simply by doing what it took to put my name on the ballot (in what appeared to be a near-hopeless cause), others were heartened to take steps that might reverberate in the halls of government for generations to come.

A lot of people online have accused me of just wanting to be a rock star in a time when there were no other concerts happening. Most of the people saying this have never been to one of our events and refuse to experience the freedom and power of God firsthand. I really believe the testimonies and results speak for themselves. I believe that Let Us Worship is part of a chorus of worship and prayer that will crescendo through the generations until Christ's return. Hopefully, one of the results of this pandemic is that the Church will be shaken out of her complacency.

In Acts 2, we see how the Church was birthed from the disciples' boldness to stand up with Peter against governmental authorities as he proclaimed the fullness of the Gospel for the first time. Peter could not remain silent, because what Jesus had come to do had been accomplished. The torch had been passed to them to carry on the work Jesus had established. Peter's bold words and the disciples' example paved the way for three thousand new disciples to come to faith that day who "devoted themselves to the apostles' teaching and to fellowship, to the breaking of bread and to prayer" (Acts 2:42).

Everywhere we gathered, we met pastors who were encouraged to go back to discipling their church members in the boldness they had received. Many new believers accepted Jesus in response to our altar calls, and the pastors excitedly reported "the fruit that remains" (John 15:16). When the government tried to shut down their churches with each new variant of the virus, they stood their ground and were filled with boldness to continue meeting together.

In California alone, the governor was sued five times for fining churches and for trying to shut down in-person services; he lost all five cases in the U.S. Supreme Court.[2] The state was ordered to repay churches $1.35 million for fines previously levied against them.[3] This precedent will make it practically impossible for the government in California to ever again forbid churches from gathering for services.

Bold stands like these create bold disciples—but they are not without cost. We are in the midst of a spiritual war between the forces of Heaven and Hell—and many people are not yet awake to this reality. There are demonic powers and principalities that want the voice of the Church to be silenced. Though we have been protected so far, it's not without real risk to our reputations, families, and even our lives. When Stephen stood up to proclaim Jesus despite a governmental mandate against doing so in his time (see Acts 6:8–8:1), the church saw immense growth again, as well as the conversion of Saul of Tarsus, who would go from being a prime persecutor of the Church to one of its greatest heroes.

Stephen lost his life for his words, but as missionary Jim Elliot famously said, "He is no fool who gives what he cannot keep to gain what he cannot lose."[4] Stephen will forever be remembered for what he did as the first martyr of the Church. Likewise, Jim Elliot and four other young missionaries were martyred in the jungles of Ecuador by warriors of the Auca people. Later, Jim's widow, Elisabeth Elliot, would return to the very same place and preach the Gospel to the very men who killed her husband. Think on that for a moment. What commitment![5]

Scripture refers several times to Jesus sitting at the right hand of the Father. But when Stephen stood up for Him, we have one of the only examples of Jesus standing up at the right hand of His Father to applaud. (See Acts 7:56.) Stephen remains one of the greatest examples of bold witness to us all.

Never underestimate the power of standing up for Jesus. Never doubt the transformative power of praying in His name. Even in defeat, when we lift Him up, He stands up with us (just like he did for Stephen)—and all who see what we did will remember it and be changed.

THIRTEEN

BOLD LEGACY

But the steadfast love of the Lord is from everlasting
to everlasting on those who fear him,
and his righteousness to children's children.

—Psalm 103:17 ESV

During our gathering on the steps of the California Capitol in Sacramento in September 2020, I announced we would be going to the National Mall in Washington, D.C. just weeks later, even though we didn't even have a permit for that date yet. We had no guarantee, no money raised, and no firm plan on how we were going to pull it off, but I had the date in my heart—October 25, 2020—because Hebrews 10:25 says we are: "not giving up meeting together, as some are in the habit of doing, but encouraging one another."

This verse had provided much-needed clarity and a theological foundation for our continued desire to host worship and prayer gatherings during a season of lockdown and fear. October 25 was also the only date the National Park Service had approved for the National Mall, and that fact brought even more confirmation that this was God's plan. I really wanted to go to the most iconic real estate in America to host our most epic gathering. This would be the crescendo of 2020. It would also be just a week and a half before the 2020 presidential election—the perfect place and timing to pray for the nation.

Of course, the National Mall is probably one of the most difficult venues in the U.S. to secure a permit for. I believe it is the most historic setting in America, with the Capitol behind it and the Washington Monument and the Lincoln Memorial Reflecting Pool in front of it. What made me even more determined to pursue this special place was my own history here.

Almost twenty years earlier, on Labor Day weekend in 2000, I attended The Call D.C., hosted by Lou Engle—a powerful intercessor with a growly voice who has now become a spiritual father to me. I was a passionate seventeen-year-old, and I gathered with more than 450,000 other people to pray, worship, fast, and seek God for revival for America. It was a moment that ignited my heart and further defined the calling of the Lord on my life.

I had spent the summer leading up to that day mobilizing youth groups, churches, and ministries across the East Coast to respond to The Call. Although no "big names" were used to promote the event (though many big names were part of it) and no social media existed at the time to drive it, there was spiritual momentum attached to that event unlike anything I had ever felt before. It was a consecrated event, and we all felt we could not afford to miss it! This was the day that God began to lay a burden on my heart to fight for the unborn and the injustice of abortion that had become a "death decree" over America since January 1973.

None of us, however, had any idea about all of the things that would take place on or near the National Mall leading up to October 25. A few months before our gathering there, Supreme Court Justice Ruth Bader Ginsburg died, and Amy Coney Barrett was nominated by President Donald Trump to take her place. The Church had been persistently praying for decades to reverse *Roe v. Wade*, and now we prayed that she was the "Esther" that God would raise up to bring deliverance to those who never get a chance to live. The U.S. Senate was in the final moments of her confirmation hearing late into the night before our event. And, of course, with the 2020 presidential election just a week away, there was more heightened activity in both the spiritual and the natural realms than anything I had experienced twenty years earlier.

The next morning, the temperature was in the low forties and raining on and off as we set up. It was the worst kind of weather for the East Coast at that time of year, and the very kind we had been praying so hard against in the previous days. Although it was not ideal, we had come too far to give up or be disheartened. After enduring the 111-degree heat with smoke in Sacramento, the flash bombs, bear spray, and blood from Antifa in Seattle, and the downpour of rain in Chicago, a little cold drizzle wasn't going to stop us in Washington, D.C.! I also knew only the gritty and wild worshippers would show up, and that is exactly the kind we needed for the National Mall.

We started hearing rumblings online that commercial flights from the West Coast were almost entirely full of worshippers coming to flood the District of Columbia with praise. Planes from San Francisco, Seattle, Portland, and Los Angeles were packed, and the people on them did not wait to reach the East Coast to start ministering to others. Prayer teams were forming mid-flight, and many people started praying for each other before they touched down in D.C.

Leading up to our main event on the National Mall that afternoon, we held a series of prayer meetings all over the city. We began at the Supreme Court that morning, where more than 3,500 people gathered in the rain together. The Capitol Police later told me it was the largest prayer meeting on record there. We then moved to St. John's Episcopal Church—known as the "church of the presidents"—which protestors had set on fire a few months before we arrived. We focused many of our prayers on the White House as well, as it was also visible from that location.

The last event before we headed to the National Mall took place on the steps of the Lincoln Memorial, the spot where Martin Luther King, Jr. delivered his famous "I Have a Dream" speech. In that location, we repented of the racial divide, humbly asked for healing, and held hands together as one Body of Christ. It was one of the most powerful moments of the entire day.

The District was completely flooded that day with Let Us Worship revivalists. They filled hotels, restaurants, coffee shops, and memorials. You could not go a block or two without seeing someone wearing one of our shirts or hoodies. Plus, the city was pretty quiet that day except for us. Professional sports were shut down. Only a very few churches were even holding services. There were no concerts or conventions taking place anywhere in the area. In the midst of a relatively empty news cycle—except for updates on the pandemic and the latest information on Amy Coney Barrett's confirmation—all eyes were on the Washington Mall to see what God was about to do.

While we had faced tremendous resistance from state and local governments in many areas, there was none in D.C. because we were on federal property. The COVID rules and shutdowns across the D.C. metropolitan region did not affect the federal agency that managed the National Mall, and President Trump was still in office at the time, so no one could raise enough noise to cancel our permit this time. (Although that did not keep the mayor from trying!) The National Park Service was very supportive of our free-speech rights under the U.S. Constitution. Officials reminded us of a few COVID protocols that were in place, as well as how long we could play and how loud it could be, but those were the only restrictions they put on us. They really treated us with respect and fairness.

That's not to say we didn't have any opposition from the outside, though. There were some protestors and some Satanists—maybe the same ones who had failed outside Gas Works Park, but who really knows?—who again showed up with bowls of blood, planning to throw it on me and the band while we were on stage. When they were unable to get close enough, and then couldn't find us as we got off the stage, they started looking for another leader who had been on stage during the event. They found Dr. Charles Karuku from Minneapolis and threw blood all over him.[1] Luckily, he was wearing a rain jacket, but that didn't keep them from getting much of it all over his face.

His reaction was the same as every other time we had faced resistance together across America. He proclaimed, "The Lord is powerful—He is mightier than this.... No weapon formed against us will prosper. Every tongue that rises in judgment will be condemned....

Keep us in prayer. We cannot be silenced by this kind of violence and intimidation, in Jesus's name, Amen!"[2]

Media reports described that night as the largest church service in America in 2020, with approximately forty thousand bold and passionate worshippers showing up in the rain for the event. When I asked from the stage how many had come from the West Coast, I was stunned to see at least 50 percent of the hands go up from all over the massive crowd. Some U.S. senators joined us after the Barrett confirmation hearings and prayed with us. When we gave the altar call, people again flooded forward to be saved and set free!

Another wild thing that happened was that while it rained on and off during the event, it seemed that no one near the front of the stage or on the sides got drenched. My wife and kids were halfway back in the middle of the crowd; they could see the rain falling, yet somehow it did not fall on them. We still have no idea what happened, but many other people reported experiencing the same thing.

We ended the four-hour time of worship, prayer, preaching, and altar calls with me standing in front of the Capitol, alone with my acoustic guitar, singing "There Is a Name." We livestreamed this special moment, bringing an online audience to the seat of our nation's government right along with us.[3] The chorus felt like exactly the right words to end with:

> *Jesus, enthroned upon the praises of our hearts*
> *Jesus, You're the King and You're the center of it all…*

It was a powerful moment—one of the most powerful and meaningful of my entire life.

Twenty years after I had taken part in an event on the Mall to lift up the name of Jesus, here I was, doing it again. We could not believe that we were in that moment, in the middle of a pandemic, in the middle of fear, in the middle of resistance, and the Lord was again gathering His people to call for revival across the land. It felt like our way of saying, "No matter how dark it is, no matter how difficult it is, no matter how impossible it seems, we believe Your words, Lord." It felt like it released a much-needed shot of faith into the soul of the nation and empowered people to believe in the dream of God, even in the midst of a very difficult time.

I believe we were also planting seeds for the next generation to carry that torch forward in an even greater way.

For the Next Generation

In the time of Nehemiah—a layman about whom little is known, except that he was serving in the court of Persian King Artaxerxes II—Israel was a wasteland. The jewel of David's kingdom, Jerusalem, lay in heaps of rubble after being destroyed by the Babylonians seventy years earlier. The protective wall of the city had been broken down and its gates burnt to ashes. In response to this, God moved Nehemiah's heart and he prayed:

Lord, the God of heaven, the great and awesome God, who keeps his covenant of love with those who love him and keep his commandments, let your ear be attentive and your eyes open to hear the prayer your servant is praying before you day and night....

Remember the instruction you gave your servant Moses, saying, "If you are unfaithful, I will scatter you among the nations, but if you return to me and obey my commands, then even if your exiled people are at the farthest horizon, I will gather them from there and bring them to the place I have chosen as a dwelling for my Name." (Nehemiah 1:5, 8–9)

Nehemiah prayed for favor with the king of Persia that he might be able to go to Jerusalem and rebuild the city. God granted him this favor, and Nehemiah obtained letters from the king giving him permission to begin the reconstruction.

You might think that would have been enough. He had the Lord's blessing and the king's letters of permission, so surely he would be able to carry out his mission without much fuss. But that wasn't the case. From the minute he started his work, he faced ridicule and fierce opposition from two local officials: Sanballat, who was Samarian, and Tobiah the Ammonite. You don't have to read much into the text to feel that these two men saw Nehemiah as a threat to their authority, and severely wanted to "put him in his place."

When Sanballat heard that we were rebuilding the wall, he became angry and was greatly incensed. He ridiculed the Jews, and in the presence of his associates and the army of Samaria, he said, "What are those feeble Jews doing? Will they restore their wall? Will they offer sacrifices? Will they finish in a day? Can they bring the stones back to life from those heaps of rubble—burned as they are?"

Tobiah the Ammonite, who was at his side, said, "What they are building—even a fox climbing up on it would break down their wall of stones!" (Nehemiah 4:1–3)

These hecklers incessantly mocked Nehemiah and his work, but he knew he had a call from the Lord to rebuild the city and to reunify his people. Under his direction, the Hebrews persisted and rebuilt the wall around Jerusalem until it was about half the height it had been before. This took great effort and determination, but the Scriptures tell us that "the people worked with all of their heart" (Nehemiah 4:6). They did not allow the mob to silence them, back them into a corner, or slow them down.

Meanwhile, the opposition upped the ante. "They all plotted together to come and fight against Jerusalem and stir up trouble against it" (Nehemiah 4:8).

In response, Nehemiah encouraged his people: "Don't be afraid of them. Remember the Lord, who is great and awesome, and fight for your families, your sons and your daughters, your wives and your homes" (Nehemiah 4:14). Knowing that what they were doing mattered greatly to the generations to follow, they armed themselves and went back to work. They took turns standing guard over their neighbors as each rebuilt the wall around his own house. The situation finally got so gnarly that everyone built with one hand and held a weapon in the other, should the opposition attack them.

Seeing that their protests and threats did no good, the hecklers began demanding that Nehemiah explain what he was doing. They invited him to meet, but the meetings were all traps. Nehemiah responded, "I am carrying on a great project and cannot go down. Why should the work stop while I leave it and go down to you?"

(Nehemiah 6:3). Four times they demanded he meet with them, and four times Nehemiah sent back the same response. The fifth time, they included a letter saying they were going to charge him with treason against the king if he did not obey.

Rather than falling for their scheme, Nehemiah called their bluff. "Nothing like what you are saying is happening; you are just making it up out of your head," he told them (Nehemiah 6:8).

Then they hired men to warn Nehemiah that an ambush had been planned and he and the Israelites should lock themselves into the temple for protection. Nehemiah refused again. "Should a man like me run away? Or should someone like me go into the temple to save his life? I will not go!" (Nehemiah 6:11). Because Nehemiah stayed focused and repelled the attacks of these instigators, the Israelites finished the work of rebuilding the wall around Jerusalem in fifty-two days through sheer grit, determination, and a long-term mindset. Bear in mind that they were still cutting stones by hand and hauling them from quarries in that age. This was a complete miracle!

I tell you this story because, honestly, so much of what we went through to hold many of our Let Us Worship gatherings across America in 2020 felt like that. To have our permits canceled with no forewarning, to have to relocate at the last minute time and again, to have the police sent when they had far better things to do, and constantly being cast as violators, disrespectful of government, superspreaders, frauds, attention-seekers, and money-grubbers—not to mention the death threats that came to my family, or the attacks and assaults on the worshippers that came to our events. Through all that, I think I know how Nehemiah felt.

We were doing something to build a legacy of faith for the generations to come—activities protected by our laws and Constitution—so to meet such incredible resistance showed us there was something deeper behind it, something darker and much more sinister in nature than politics and power games.

Many things have been said about the Let Us Worship movement, but one of the things the Lord impressed on us as we prayed for the D.C. gathering was that we were building something for the next generation to carry forward. The phrase that came to us as we began praying was "Gen Z for Jesus." In fact, my ten-year-old daughter Keturah came to the stage to pray as a representative of the generations to come.[4] It was as Jesus said, quoting the Psalms: "Out of the mouth of babes and sucklings thou hast perfected praise" (Matthew 21:16 KJV). Her voice and prayer moved everyone there. Standing on the stage beside me, Keturah prayed:

Dear Jesus,

I just pray for my generation to be more in love with You, to know more of You, to experience You more, because, God, You're so good—You're still good! And I know that things are going to be different, so different.

I pray for the cross to make a way. I pray for revival to hit, and I just saw everyone just opening a gift from God. I feel like everyone is going to get a beautiful gift from the Holy Spirit. I just pray for more of that. I'm just gonna, yeah, blast that over everyone. I just feel everyone flowing, everyone flowing in Your presence. I pray for more of that, because You're so good! You're amazing!

A new Jesus People Movement is here! This is what we had prayed for and boldly declared on the Golden Gate Bridge earlier that year. This movement must extend to the next generation if it is going to change the nation and the world.

We knew it was our calling to do as Psalm 145:4 says,

> One generation commends your works to another;
> they tell of your mighty acts.

It is up to us as spiritual mothers and fathers to do as Nehemiah did, in the face of opposition, questioning, and threats: we need to rebuild the walls of revival in our families, cities, and nations. Our ceiling must become the next generation's floor. We want them to be able to go higher, faster, and farther than we ever dreamed!

As an extension of that, when we returned to the Golden Gate Bridge in July 2021 for the one-year anniversary of Let Us Worship, we turned over the worship at the end to a group of teens and twentysomethings. A young, upcoming worship leader named Joel Mott had attended one of our early events, where he got inspired to do the same thing we were doing with the next generation. Joel began to gather people in high schools, colleges, universities, and on beaches for Let-Us-Worship-like events. At first, the groups were small, but then they began to grow. They began conducting outreach and evangelism at every gathering they did. We were so proud of them.

When we handed the worship over to them at the anniversary event, they rose to the occasion and brought Heaven to Earth in the park that day. They sang, they preached, they gave altar calls, they ministered to people. They went all out.

Where we had had about four hundred join us at Golden Gate Park in 2020, we had well over 1,500 join us on the bridge in 2021; we held hands, and our group nearly spanned the entire channel. By the time we landed in Golden Gate Park afterward to pray some more, there were nearly four thousand of us. It was great to see the next generation of believers leading such a large group with such zeal for the Lord. What a blessing to watch that moment happen!

Yes, what we do in our lives is important for today—there are many lives that need to be touched and pulled out of all kinds of darkness—but at the same time, we need to remember what we are establishing for tomorrow. It's not really about us or our ministries. That is all short-term thinking. It's not about building our social media followings. If we build something huge but it doesn't last beyond us, we're missing the point.

What it *is* about is God igniting the hearts of the next generation. They must carry the fire! That will be the ultimate fruit of the Let Us Worship movement—that what we began in the midst of the sickness, isolation, hopelessness, and frustration of the COVID-19 pandemic will infect the next generation with the faith, hope, and love of Jesus Christ as the answer to whatever we face. It's a fight for the here and now, but it's also a fight for our sons, our daughters, our families, and our nation in the decades to come. We must work with one hand and have the other raised in worship and prayer. That's the imprint we want to leave, and we hope it lasts until the generation that welcomes Jesus back home.

That is what Let Us Worship fought for and hopefully has accomplished. And it is our prayer for the generations to come.

FOURTEEN

BOLD HOPE

Against all hope, Abraham in hope believed and so became the father of many nations.

—Romans 4:18

Almost as soon as we got back home to the West Coast after the amazing and rainy D.C. event, we determined we wanted to gather there again the next year. This would be our annual flagship event. We immediately started applying for a permit, but things seemed even more locked down in early 2021 than they had been in 2020. The National Park Service refused to give us a date. We kept going back and forth with them, trying to nail down a date that would work, and agents kept saying nothing was available. Even though there was nothing on the books, for some reason it seemed they could not schedule us.

So, like the widow going before the unjust judge (see Luke 18:1–8), we just kept asking. We emailed the NPS almost every week, continuing to ask.

I don't know if something legitimately changed or they just gave up so we would stop annoying them, but finally, NPS came back with the dates of September 11 and 12—the twentieth anniversary of the 9/11 attacks—as possibilities for when we could hold another gathering on the National Mall. We couldn't believe it. Out of all the possible dates in the fall, how could there not be some other larger event going on to commemorate that tragedy?

Then we realized that if God had provided us these dates, maybe we could be the ones to host the commemoration on the most special real estate in America, the National Mall. We really felt like the Lord was giving us those dates for something monumental—that this time of mourning, heartache, and trauma for our nation might be turned into the sacrifice of praise to God. This is how we began dreaming and planning for another historic gathering.

As you surely remember, 2021 was a difficult year for America (and the rest of the world). We continued to travel and bring worship, revival, and hope to the cities across our nation that we believed needed it most. When Joe Biden pulled our troops out of Afghanistan in late August, this sent yet another ripple of uncertainty across the land. We watched in horror as the Taliban filled the vacuum with surprising speed and many innocent people lost their lives trying to escape. Many Afghans were murdered for simply having had anything to do with Americans during the war on terror and in the days afterward. Thirteen U.S. Marines guarding the airport in Kabul were killed in a bomb attack. It was as if the wound left by the attacks of September 11, 2001, were being ripped open again, and fear and hopelessness began to sink in. This was a botched troop withdrawal of epic proportions, and many died who should not have had to pay the price for it.

I felt close ties to the people of Afghanistan because I had been there in early 2002. A friend who was rebuilding a girls' school that the Taliban had destroyed invited me to bring my guitar and come help. I was still in high school at the time, and I *still* can't believe my parents let me go!

Afghanistan dominated the news at the time, as the U.S. troops were fully settled in. My trip was incredible, and the reception and kindness of the people was something I will never forget. They really loved music, and I used it as a tool to bring unity and healing. The tribal leaders of the mountain villages sat with me every night until the stars came out, sharing stories of what they had endured under Taliban rule and how happy they were that the U.S. was now pushing the terrorists out. My time in Afghanistan as a teenager marked me and set a course to fall in love with God's heart for the Muslim world.

Over the years since the attacks on the World Trade Center, we had come to see the date of September 11 as significant because of God's 9-1-1 call, His response to tragedies on the earth, as outlined in Amos 9:11:

> In that day
> I will restore David's fallen shelter—
> I will repair its broken walls
> and restore its ruins—
> and will rebuild it as it used to be.

In response to any crisis the nation of Israel faced, the first call was to "restore David's fallen shelter." Throughout the Scriptures,

David's place of refuge was always praise and worship—whether he was in the field with his sheep, facing down Goliath, fleeing from Saul's court, sitting on the throne, mourning the death of a child, or even running from his own son's usurpation. Rebuilding the place of worship and prayer so the rest of mankind may seek the Lord is always a primary part of our first response to a tragedy, or any other time we need help from God.

With this new pain of the sudden withdrawal of troops, we felt like we were going to be in the right place at the right time again on the National Mall for the twentieth anniversary of 9/11, so we began inviting others to join us. We reached out to political leaders, military leaders, faith leaders, and many pastors from the area. Every living U.S. president since September 11, 2001, received an official invitation to join us—George W. Bush, Barack Obama, Donald Trump, and Joe Biden.

President Trump was the only one to respond. This honestly shocked me. With the date secured and our history of gathering diverse groups across America, I believed more than one of them would. But that did not happen. Rather than sulk or complain, we moved forward with President Trump; he agreed to meet with me and film an address to America that we could play that night on the National Mall. He actually said several times that he wanted to come in person, but the Secret Service advised against it.

Continuing a tradition we had established earlier, we invited all of the members of Congress, members of the Senate, and Joe Biden and Kamala Harris once again, even though very few of them ever joined us. We also decided to use the event to launch twenty-one days of prayer and fasting for revival and the healing for our nation.

The morning of September 11, 2021, we planted an American flag on the grave of every service person buried in Arlington National Cemetery who had lost their lives in the War on Terror. I do not believe this had ever happened before. We prayed for our military service members. We prayed for their families. We had military leaders on stage during the event, and we ended the night in worship, placing our dependence on God to heal our nation.

On September 12, we returned for a four-hour worship-and-prayer revival meeting that was one of the most powerful we have ever done. Let Us Worship had grown in size, impact, and wisdom over the months since we had last been in D.C. We were carrying the hopes and prayers of 120 cities with us when we gathered on the National Mall that day! Once again, in the face of darkness and the trauma of the past, the pain of the events in Afghanistan, and everything America was still experiencing as new variants of COVID-19 sent shockwaves of fear through the nation, we lifted up the name of Jesus, declaring "the garment of praise for the spirit of heaviness" (Isaiah 61:3 KJV).

As we had in 2020, we held prayer meetings earlier in the day on the key sites in our nation's capital leading up to the event on the Mall—the steps of the Supreme Court, in front of the White House, and the Lincoln Memorial—and worshipped and prayed. Once again, my daughter Keturah (now eleven years old) lifted up a powerful prayer over the White House:

> I pray that the Holy Spirit will hit the White House right now. I just see a light switch—you know, when you turn the lights on. I feel that God is turning the lights on because it's dark, but He turns the darkness

into light. He turns the fear into, like, peace, faith. And I just declare over the White House, over Joe Biden, over everyone that's scared in there, that they'll just feel Heaven come down on them right now. In Jesus's name, Amen![1]

In the darkest and most difficult, tumultuous times, the Lord's calling on us is always to be a people of bold hope. Because we know His hope, He expects us to carry hope, to bring hope, and to release hope. That's exactly what happened in that moment on the National Mall in 2021. It turned into a celebratory gathering where we began to dream with God, and believe and expect that amazing things were going to happen in this season, regardless of the darkness we had endured.

It's time for those of us who know where the switch is to turn on the light for our churches, our communities, and our nation.

It All Starts with Hope

In Chapter One, I quoted Hebrews 11:1 (KJV): "Faith is the substance of things hoped for, the evidence of things not seen." Another way to say this is that, without hope, faith has nothing to give substance to. There's no room for faith in hopelessness. Things are only dark when there is no light—any light at all will chase darkness into the shadows and out the door. That's the reason that hope is just as important as faith and love, because it is the beginning point. Hope makes faith possible, and faith expresses itself through love. (See Galatians 5:6.)

Hope allows us to raise our eyes, as the psalmist said,

I lift up my eyes to the mountains—
where does my help come from?
My help comes from the Lord,
the Maker of heaven and earth. (Psalm 122:1–2)

We live in an age when hopelessness is a plague. The enemy doesn't want people to know there is a God in order to keep them from hoping for a better life. Also, many in our culture want to convince you that you are your own god. The spirit behind this tries to control and manipulate us so that we are left with little of anything, even dignity. We often point to corruption and crime as problems (which they are), but all of this originates in hopelessness. Someone who has hope of a meal tomorrow doesn't steal bread today. Someone who has a hope of building a good life for themselves and their family through legitimate means doesn't embezzle or steal. A person who knows the hope of reconciliation doesn't murder. Stealing someone's hope may well be the most insidious thing in the world to do.

In giving hope, I don't mean we should deny reality, as some seem to do, either. False hope can often be worse than no hope at all, because when it proves empty, the person is less likely to trust in hope again. But real hope stares reality in the face and refuses to be beaten by it.

As I have said before, I am not a COVID denier. Many of my family members work in the medical community, and some of my close friends and heroes have died from COVID. It's no joke, and it is a real virus—but it's also not unbeatable, nor is it more powerful than God. The medical community continues to fight it; wisdom will win out; and people of faith should not let it put us in a box or stop us from expressing our faith in worship, prayer, and declaring who God is in the midst of it all.

Many scriptures in the Bible call Abraham "the father of faith" and point to him as an example for us. Paul tells us in Romans:

> Against all hope, Abraham in hope believed and so became the father of many nations, just as it had been said to him, "So shall your offspring be." (Romans 4:18)

God had told Abraham that he would be the father of many nations, but for many years, as you probably know, Abraham had no children. In fact, he was 100 years old and his wife Sarah was ninety, and they still didn't have any kids. Scripture tells us that Abraham knew the conditions of their bodies but chose instead to believe God more than the aches and pains of age that he felt every day.

> Without weakening in his faith, he faced the fact that his body was as good as dead—since he was about a hundred years old—and that Sarah's womb was also dead. Yet he did not waver through unbelief regarding the promise of God, but was strengthened in his faith and gave glory to God, being fully persuaded that God had power to do what he had promised. (Romans 4:19–21)

We didn't go to Washington, D.C., on September 11, 2021, denying the pain and trauma of the attacks on our soil and the battles that have been fought around the world since then. Good men and women have lost their lives to the fight to stop terrorists from taking the lives and freedoms of those they oppress. We've done what little we can to meet some needs in the Middle East through our ministries, but at the same time, we know the best and most powerful thing we can bring is the Gospel and the presence of God to the oppressed, which can alter mindsets and change hearts.

Jesus is always the doorway to hope, and all great and lasting breakthrough begins there. An inherent optimism surrounds our hearts and minds when we think about what God has already done and is capable of doing if we will learn to trust in and follow Him.

Knowing these things deeply allows us to be people of bold hope. It gives us the courage to do things everyone around us find crazy because they are so often countercultural. It seems otherworldly because, frankly, it is.

So I encourage you to be willing to be bold in hope. It is vulnerable and even scary at times, but it is our greatest reality when times are tough. Where there is darkness, it is time to light a candle. When you are up against a wall, lift up your eyes to the hills, looking for the help only God can provide. You may feel alone, but you are not. God sees you, knows you, and is only a prayer away. He is always our source of hope, and always gives a word of hope we can share with others. Keep up the good fight of hope. God is counting on each of us to do our part. He is indeed the greatest hope for the world we live in.

The call to boldness should not be taken lightly, but it is one any of us can answer. It doesn't start with stepping onto a stage or shouting the Gospel on your social media accounts. True boldness doesn't come from bravado; it's built on conviction. It comes first by entering the door of salvation, but then going further in to know Jesus for who He was in the Bible and who He is in your life today.

First, embrace the Bible as God's personal word to you. 2 Peter 1:3 in *The Message* paraphrase says it this way: "Everything that goes into a life of pleasing God has been miraculously given to us by getting to know, personally and intimately, the One who invited us to God." To that end, God wrote us a nice long letter—the Bible—so that we could get to know Him and the Son He would send to save us.

Second, talk with God. Prayer is not the practice of reading a laundry list of needs and then saying, "In Jesus's name, amen." It is a conversation with God. It is soaking in His Presence. It is asking the hardest questions we know to ask, and then answering them together with Him through study and further prayer. Many mistake the call of God on their lives as something they are supposed to do *for* Him, as if He is an employer who needs to get things done so His business will succeed. That's missing the point. God gives big dreams and callings because He doesn't want us to rely on our own strength. He asks us to do things that are so far beyond us that we dare not attempt them without counting on Him every step of the way.

He hasn't, for example, called me to be a worship leader because He needs the adoration. He loves to show up during worship events because it's a chance for Him to be with His kids. It's a chance for Him to be present in *our* midst. That's just the kind of Father He is.

Third, as you have read again and again throughout this book, "Do not forsake gathering together as some have done." (See Hebrews 10:25.) Certainly, there have been some obstacles to doing so in this COVID era, especially for some with health challenges of different kinds, but those are falling away. Even if you are only online, show up for church, show up for Bible study, gather together, and pray! If you can attend outdoor meetings your church is having, do so. Organize impromptu worship gatherings on your own. Show up when your church is serving food to the hungry or doing outreach in your community. Remember the key ingredients of what the Bible says and live them out loud. God has called each of us to do those things, and they are how we grow bolder together.

Fourth, follow the words of Scripture that appear hundreds of times throughout the Bible: "Fear not." Don't make decisions based on fear. Make decisions based on faith. That is one of the reasons it's so important to know God for who He really is.

In the end, the key to boldness is being unapologetically who God has called you to be in your faith, your prayers, your worship, your mission, your leadership, your love, your justice, your obedience, your gratitude, your identity, your witness, your unity, your legacy, and your hope. A cold world needs the hot fire of bold believers.

> You are the light of the world. A town built on a hill cannot be hidden. Neither do people light a lamp and put it under a bowl. Instead they put it on its stand, and it gives light to everyone in the house. In the same way, let your light shine before others, that they may see your good deeds and glorify your Father in heaven. (Matthew 5:14–16)

NOTES

One: Bold Faith

1. Jennifer A. Kingson, "Exclusive: $1 Billion-Plus Riot Damage Is Most Expensive in Insurance History," Axios, September 16, 2020, https://www.axios.com/riots-cost-property-damage-276c9bcc-a455 -4067-b06a-66f9db4cea9c.html.

2. California Department of Public Health and State of California Department of Industrial Relations, "COVID-19 Industry Guidance: Places of Worship and Providers of Religious Services and Cultural Ceremonies," Covid19.ca.gov, July 29, 2020, 3, https://files.covid19 .ca.gov/pdf/guidance-places-of-worship.pdf.

Two: Bold Prayers

1. Life To The Fullest, "A New Jesus People Movement ‖ Golden Gate Bridge Worship with Sean Feucht, Stand Up for Our Freedom," YouTube, July 21, 2020, https://www.youtube.com/watch?v=SFtEb UlX81w.

Three: Bold Worship

1. "One in Three Practicing Christians Has Stopped Attending Church during COVID-19," Barna.com, July 8, 2020, https://www.barna .com/research/new-sunday-morning-part-2/.

Five: Bold Leadership

1. Tori Lieberman, "New FBI Figures Show Portland Is Way above Average in Its Increased Rate of Homicides," *Willamette Week*, September 9, 2021, https://www.wweek.com/news/2021/09/29/new -fbi-figures-show-portland-is-way-above-average-in-its-increased-ra te-of-homicides/.

Six: Bold Love

1. Evie Fordham, "Seattle CHOP Zone Businesses Worry about Slow Police Response Times," FoxBusiness, June 16, 2020, https://www .foxbusiness.com/money/chop-zone-seattle-businesses-police.

2. Katelyn Burns, "The Violent End of the Capitol Hill Organized Protest, Explained," Vox, July 2, 2020, https://www.vox.com/policy -and-politics/2020/7/2/21310109/chop-chaz-cleared-violence-expla ined.

3. Julia Duin, "'This Is All About Jesus': A Christian Rocker's Covid Protest Movement," *Politico*, October 25, 2020, https://www.politi co.com/news/magazine/2020/10/25/sean-feucht-christian-rocker-co vid-protest-movement-431734.

Nine: Bold Gratitude

1. Sean Feucht, "Let Us Worship – Live from Sacramento – Full Concert Film," YouTube, September 20, 2020, https:// www.youtube.com/watch?v=lPbR-xccRkU.

2. Willie Nelson, *The Tao of Willie: A Guide to the Happiness in Your Heart* (New York: Gotham Books, 2006), loc 185, Kindle.

3. Alex M. Wood, Jeffrey J. Froh, and Adam W. A. Geraghty, "Gratitude and Well-Being: A Review and Theoretical Integration," *Clinical Psychology Review* (November 2010), doi:10.1016/j.cpr.2010.03.005.

Eleven: Bold Unity

1. Joseph Hudak, "Jesus Christ, Superspreader?: Preacher-Musician Sean Feucht Stages Nashville Concert, Ignoring Covid-19 Precautions," *Rolling Stone*, October 12, 2020, https://www.rollingstone.com/culture/culture-news/sean-feucht-preacher-covid-1074213.

2. Tiffany Baptiste, "Singer Lauren Daigle Responds to Mayor's Call to Be Pulled from New Year's Eve Performance," Fox8live.com, December 18, 2020, https://www.fox8live.com/2020/12/18/singer-lauren-daigle-responds-mayors-call-be-pulled-new-years-eve-performance/.

Twelve: Bold Witness

1. Ryan Foley, "LA Mission to Hold New Year's Eve Celebration, Push for 'Christian Unity,'" *Christian Post*, December 30, 2020, https://www.christianpost.com/news/la-mission-to-hold-nye-celebration-push-for-christian-unity.html.

2. Emily Hoeven, "Newsom Loses Biggest Court Battle Yet," Cal Matters, February 8, 2021, https://calmatters.org/newsletters/what matters/2021/02/churches-can-reopen-indoors-california/.

3. Brie Stimson, "California's Newsom Order to Pay $1.35M in Settlements with LA-Area Church over Coronavirus Restrictions,"

Fox News, May 26, 2021, https://www.foxnews.com/politics/gavin-newsom-to-pay-1-35-million-in-settlement-with-la-church-over-co ronavirus-restrictions.

4. Justin Taylor, "He Was No Fool," *The Gospel Coalition* (blog), January 9, 2010, https://www.thegospelcoalition.org/blogs/justin-ta ylor/he-ws-no-fool/.

5. Joe Carter, "9 Things You Should Know about Elizabeth Elliot," The Gospel Coalition Current Events, June 15, 2015, https://www .thegospelcoalition.org/article/9-things-you-should-know-about-elis abeth-elliot/.

Thirteen: Bold Legacy

1. CBN News, "Satanic Protestor Dumped Blood All Over Christian Preacher at Washington Prayer Event," CBNNews.com, October 26, 2020, https://www1.cbn.com/cbnnews/us/2020/october/satani st-dumped-blood-all-over-christian-preacher-at-washington-prayer -event.

2. Ibid.

3. We don't know exactly how many people joined us online that night, but so far, the recording of that evening has been viewed more than 750,000 times through social media.

4. You can hear this on the worship album we recorded at that event, *Let Us Worship—Washington, D.C.*, which hit number one on Apple Music across all genres.

Fourteen: Bold Hope

1. Sean Feucht, "#LETUSWORSHIP – Sean Feucht – Washington, D.C. – 2021," YouTube, September 13, 2021, https://www.you tube.com/watch?v=hwrWY7HuhBU.

MEET SEAN

Sean Feucht is a speaker, author, missionary, artist, activist, and the founder of multiple global movements including Burn 24-7, a worship and prayer movement now spanning six continents and more than 250 cities; Light A Candle, a global missions and compassion movement bringing light, hope, healing, and tangible love to the hardest, darkest, and most isolated places of the earth; Hold the Line, a movement seeking to engage the church and young people to inform, educate, and inspire the next generation of leaders to stand for what is right in the governmental arena; and Let Us Worship, a movement across America gathering believers to worship and pray boldly for revival. Let Us Worship albums have seen great success, four reaching number one on iTunes in Christian Worship, and three albums (*Let Us Worship—Azusa, Let Us Worship—Washington, D.C.,* and *Let Us Worship—Awake America*) ranking number one over every genre in the world for multiple days in a row on iTunes.

Sean is married to his high school sweetheart, Kate, and is obsessed with their four children: Keturah, Malachi, Ezra, and Zion. His heart is to bring integrity, hope, and inspiration to every sphere of society. His lifelong quest and dream is to witness a generation of burning hearts arise across the nations of the world with renewed faith, vision, and sacrificial pursuit of the Presence of God.